"Frances Miles has written a c[o] book that will be various[ly] challenging, and cathartic for its readers. Her own journeying of self-discovery and the winsome stories of many others are interwoven with biblical insights to share — and potentially transform."
Rev. Dr Martyn Atkins

"Faces on old family photos, with names we may not even remember — what's their legacy to us? And what will our legacy be for generations to come? This thoughtful book helps us to understand ourselves by getting to know the character, circumstances, and convictions of those who came before us."
Pam Rhodes,
TV and Radio Presenter

"Frances Miles has achieved something quite refreshing — presenting personal reflection and life situations in a way that allows readers to recognise themselves or the emotions involved. She offers insight, spiritual devotion, biblical reflection, and fun! It's just the kind of book to read while contemplating life, the universe and everything."
Rev. Dr G. Howard Mellor

"Love. What subject could be more important? Frances sensitively explores the subject of 'belonging' to each other and our Father God through various interesting stories. She also suggests simple things we can all do to say to others 'I love you.'"
Jacqui Parkinson,
Textile Artist, 'Threads Through the Bible'

"Hidden deep within each one of us is the need to know we belong. Often it goes unspoken, but it's there. Engaging and practical, Frances addresses this important theme with insight and compassion. Bringing a message of hope for us and those in our circle and care."
Dave Bilborough,
Worship Leader and Songwriter

"At last, a straightforward, clearly written book focusing on Fatherhood as the key to identity. Bravo, Frances! I'm thrilled you've written what God placed on your heart years ago. I suspect it may never make it to my bookshelf but instead serve as a vital resource in my life toolkit."
Diane-Louise Jordan,
Broadcaster

"Frances shares with honesty and vulnerability the importance of relationships and our need to know both who we are and whom we belong to. With insights to meditate on and practical next steps, this book will help us all become more fully alive."
Andy Frost,
Director of Share Jesus International

"'Rooted, Loved, Affirmed' is an acutely personal account dealing with life, touching relationships and rooted in the spiritual. Frances Miles explores the importance of identity and heritage, validation and acknowledgement, family and faith. It is woven through with rich nuggets and threads of insight, considering aspects of 'Who am I?' It was a compelling read, leaving me wanting more."
Jonathan Clark,
Director of Premier Lifeline

Rooted
Loved
Affirmed

Imperfect Lives Encountering Perfect Love

Copyright © 2025 Frances Miles

The moral right of the author has been asserted.

Apart from any fair dealing for the purposes of research or private study, or criticism or review, as permitted under Copyright, Design and Patents Act 1998, this publication may only be reproduced, stored or transmitted, in any form or by any means, with prior permission in writing of the publishers, or in any case of the reprographic reproduction in accordance with the terms of licences issued by the Copyright Licensing Agency. Enquiries concerning reproduction outside these terms should be sent to the publishers.

PublishU Ltd

www.PublishU.com

Scripture from the Holy Bible, New International Version®, NIV®.

Copyright © 1973, 1978, 1984, 2011 by Biblica, Inc.™ Used by permission of Zondervan. All rights reserved worldwide.

All rights of this publication are reserved.

Thanks

This book is dedicated to my parents, Ann and Michael, who loved and nurtured me and my three siblings, providing a solid foundation for our faith to grow.

It is also for my children, Hannah and Jonathan; you made me a mum, and through you, I have learned so much.

Lastly, this is for my grandchildren; you bring me so much joy! I pray that each of you will come to know that God loves you even more than Grandma and Grandad do. He will be your strongest anchor in life.

I would like to express my thanks to:

Ali, Charlie, and Cally for their insightful comments while I worked on this manuscript, as well as all those who kindly provided wise observations and words of endorsement;

Matt and the team at PublishU; and

My husband, Tony. I couldn't have achieved this without your support, love, and encouragement.

Contents

Foreword

Introduction

A Reflection Trees

Chapter 1 What's Missing?

Chapter 2 Looking for You

Chapter 3 "You are My Son..."

Chapter 4 "...Whom I Love"

Chapter 5 Love in an Imperfect World

Chapter 6 "With You I Am Well-Pleased"

Chapter 7 Fathers and Sons

Chapter 8 Mothers, Fathers, Sons and Daughters

Chapter 9 A Wider and Longer Perspective

Chapter 10 Words, Words, Words

Chapter 11 Let's Get Practical

Chapter 12 "I Just Don't Know"

Chapter 13 Words of Affirmation, A Second Time

Conclusion

References

About the Author

FRANCES MILES

Foreword

Why am I writing the foreword for this book? Well, I know the author well. Extremely well, in fact! That's because we've known each other for over 46 years and have been married for 40. Yes, I admit it's probably odd for a husband to introduce his wife's book. Still, I can vouch for her authenticity more than anyone. I have witnessed her passion for the insight she has gained through years of reading, listening and reflecting. Her thoughts have bubbled up from the deep wellsprings of her Christian faith as she has pondered and prayed.

As a family, we've known Frances — Mum/Grandma — to be a rock who is compassionate, generous and selfless in her care and concern for others. My ministry and broadcasting have meant that I am often in the public eye or in people's ears! Yet, many of my best stories, anecdotes and insights have been either inspired by Frances or she has shared with me to use in my ministry. In all this, Frances has been a constant companion, an honest critic, yet always a faithful encourager.

It is now time for her to find her own voice, and I find it refreshing to proofread her work rather than the other way around. If she were a preacher, I would say that Frances practices what she preaches. More accurately, she lovingly shares her insights rather than simply proclaiming them. Before she typed a single word of this manuscript, she was already living out her beliefs with humility, grace and integrity.

It is my prayer that this book will inspire and bless you, just as Frances has been a continual source of inspiration and blessing in my life. Unsurprisingly, next to God, she is the one who has ensured that my life, faith and ministry are 'Rooted, Loved, and Affirmed'.

Tony Miles, Methodist Minister and Broadcaster

Introduction

*"Who we are cannot be separated
from where we're from."*
Malcolm Gladwell, author and speaker

Discussions and Discoveries

On an ordinary weekday at work, I found myself engaged in a debate with my colleagues that occupied my mind and thoughts for a long time afterwards. Even though it's been over twenty years, I can still vividly recall where I stood in the room and can picture my boss, who overheard the animated discussion and came to join in, leaning against the door connecting his office to ours. We discussed something none of us had experienced, yet it was nonetheless quite impactful.

I had heard about someone who had anonymously fathered children as a donor while he was at college. Some years later, as a mature man with his own family, he wanted to trace his children to see if they were interested in connecting with him. Even without knowing the whole story, I argued that a parent wishing to reach out to their child was a positive step. I felt it was valuable that people have access to understanding more about their roots and identity and should be entitled to find out where they fit in.

My young colleagues, however, disputed this, asserting that starting down this road was too complicated and potentially risky. They believed that a lifelong anonymity agreement should remain, even if the student later changed his mind and wanted his offspring to know who he was.

I think I was regarded as old-fashioned and set in my ways. The moment passed, and we returned to our desks, but thoughts about the matter lingered, swirling around in my head and taking root in my soul.

Over the following years, I had an invisible antenna, picking up narratives from people who, for whatever reason, were feeling bereft and a bit lost because they wanted to know something about their past or their family background. The lively discussion with my very dear colleagues a long time ago led me on a journey of reflection, keeping that antenna tuned and gleaning stories of despair and hope. It's made me realise how blessed I am to have grown up in a loving nuclear family with my mum, dad and siblings. I'm acutely aware that many have not had that experience.

As a nation of over 68 million people with different circumstances, I appreciate that families come in all shapes and sizes, and there is no one-size-fits-all framework. Modern ways of working, living and relating to one another can be complicated and, at times, messy. The number of lone-parent households in the UK has increased significantly, from 570,000 in 1971 to 3.2 million in 2023. But despite all the changes and differences, we are, at the heart, one connected human family.

Fellow Travellers

Getting on a packed bus in my bustling hometown in South London, my fellow travellers and I represent all corners of the earth. We come from various backgrounds, speak different languages and embody diverse cultures, styles of dress and skin tones. Though we are all distinct, we share commonalities too. We each carry a measure of hope and fear, reflections of past regrets and joyful memories. Naturally, what also unites us is that almost everyone has their head down, intently focused on their phones! Yet that is only part of the picture — and that is where and why 'Rooted, Loved, Affirmed' turned from a twenty-year pondering into what you are reading today. I will recount some real-life stories and reflect on ideas about knowing who we are and that we are loved.

It was not just other people's lives and situations that got me thinking. I will share questions I've had in my life and how I found the answers.

Who Is This Book For?

Whether you're a parent, grandparent, aunt, uncle, older sibling or caregiver, raising a child involves many levels of responsibility, effort, joy and learning. I hope this book will be a guide to stimulate and challenge you to reflect on that crucial role. You might not have a family, but you can remember your childhood and upbringing. Perhaps it's a bit of both.

My sincere hope is that you will journey with me through the book. You might already have a strong Christian belief or just a little faith; perhaps you don't have any, but I trust something will connect with your soul, even if you disagree with me! Just for the record, I am not an expert in the subject; I don't have a formal qualification to back me up. I simply believe God laid this on my heart, and I needed to share it with others.

How to Make the Best Use of the Book

Throughout the book, I use stories from my own experience or those of others I know. I will also include those I have seen, read, or heard. These, along with the reflections and thoughts that shaped and developed my thinking, might resonate with you and your experience.

At the end of each chapter, I have included a thought for the day — something to consider or an action to take.

I am passionate about sharing what I have learned through years of reading, listening and pondering. We will begin that journey with a story about my missing pen and another about a dinner party faux pas regarding homemade Banoffee Pie.

But firstly, I want to share a reflection with you.

A Reflection: Trees

I love trees.

I might not know the name of each one, but as I walk past one on this chilly autumn morning, I marvel at the red, orange, brown and yellow leaves that are now

gently

    silently

        softly

            falling

                onto the ground.

Such beauty under my shoes obscures the plain, cold, grey suburban pavement with a golden patchwork.

I love trees.

They remain dignified and defiant on roadsides against the noise of passing traffic, standing steady and strong in parks and woodlands. They are silent witnesses to the chatter of children riding by on bicycles, the runner checking her watch, the older man with his walking stick, the young couple strolling hand in hand, and the lady with the dog. Oh, the dogs!

I love trees.

Standing tall, the bare beauty of winter branches framed against the darkening sky.

And then... in time... the bursting buds and delicate blossoms will warm my heart and excite my senses once again — spring will be on its way!

Ah yes, that fresh, bright green colour of early spring. The birds will perch safely amongst the leaves on the branches and gladly sing their songs of praise.

Yes, I love trees.

They are magnificent to look at. But lest we forget, the roots — hidden beneath our feet — are silently working, growing, seeking nutrients and keeping the tree firm and beautiful, stronger and taller than you and me.

Without those roots, the tree would be nothing. The birds would have no branches, the branches would be bereft of leaves, and there would be nothing for the children, for the men, the women... and the dogs.

There would be no height... grandeur... or beautiful canopy for shade.

The roots keep the tree secure and strong despite the storms, the droughts, the snow and the ice.

I love trees with hidden roots. They remind me of the anchors in my life that make me feel secure and allow me to stand strong and resolute against the storms of life.

Roots and trees... roots and me... and you.

FRANCES MILES

Chapter 1
What's Missing?

My husband bought me a beautiful pen for my birthday several years ago — not just an ordinary plastic biro pen. This one is made with chrome; it is lovely to look at and hold, with just the right weight and balance. I always have a pen with me whenever I go somewhere. Still, this particular pen is reserved for when I go somewhere special, i.e. not to the local store or to fill the car with petrol! I put it in my handbag with some notepaper to write something down. So far, so good. The trouble is that my precious pen went missing while I was writing this book. I have been looking through all my handbags, turning each one upside down and shaking them. I have asked various people I might have lent the pen to. I have searched through loose wrapping paper, in rubbish bins, under papers on my desk, beneath the seats in the car, and rummaged through numerous drawers. Sadly, so far, no pen.

Of course, it is replaceable, but I am sad about losing it because it is special to me. And somehow, when I use the pen, my writing is so much neater!

In contrast to my pen story, there was an occasion when I had no idea that I was missing something until it was too late.

The Dessert Had Looked Absolutely Fine From the Outside...

"Never be fooled by what you see on the outside because, on the inside, it's often a different story." — Anon.

I enjoy cookery programmes, especially those where the contestants create amazing dishes with impressive artistry and finesse. Unfortunately, for my husband and family, I don't often bake many cakes or create astounding meals. However, I do have a couple of things that I enjoy making; perhaps one of my very humble "signature dishes" for dessert is Banoffee Pie. This very popular dish was first created by a British chef working at a restaurant in Sussex, England, in 1972.

My husband is a Methodist Minister, and one evening, we were hosting a meal for some of our church's leadership team. I confidently brought out the Banoffee Pie, which I had mainly prepared the night before and finished before our visitors arrived. Perfect. As I was carefully lifting the first slice out of the dish and onto a plate, one of our guests asked: "So what goes into a Banoffee Pie?" I froze... the slice precariously balancing on the pie server, halfway between the dish and the plate.

"Well, do you know, it's funny you should ask that," I replied, half-smiling. "That's an excellent question. It should have a biscuit base with a layer of toffee-like caramel, sliced bananas, whipped cream, and chocolate sprinkled on top. Hence "Ban...offee". But now that you have asked me, I have just realised I left out the caramel filling last night when I was making it!"

We all laughed, and our guests politely ate their "delicious!" biscuit, bananas and cream.

Later that evening, a friend ridiculed me when they learnt about my mistake. He gleefully texted me, "I hear your guests enjoyed their Ban Pie." At least I provided some comedy material for a while.

The dessert looked absolutely fine from the outside. The mistake came to light only when it was being served and the question asked. Suppose Ama hadn't enquired about the ingredients. In that case, I am sure the guests, most of whom hadn't tasted banoffee pie before, wouldn't have realised anything was missing.

It can be easy to cover up what is missing or wrong in our lives. Perhaps there is something buried deep in the layers of the years that we have forgotten about ourselves or spent time trying to ignore, hoping others won't notice.

A middle-aged participant on a reality TV show was proving quite reticent when sharing his feelings. He was very defensive in his conversations. Later, he confessed, "I've got a lot of layers. I've had hurts and locked them up."

We all carry the layers of our life experiences around with us, whether consciously or not. There may be times when something brings those to mind. We can find appropriate help to tentatively and gently unlock the door to our questions, hurts and emotions. For some, this is a lifetime's journey.

"No man is an island, entire of itself; every man is a piece of the continent, a part of the main." — John Donne

Missing in an Unmarked Grave

Michael is one of the children whose father served overseas in the Korean War in the 1950s. 60,000 British troops were involved in this campaign, and hundreds of them were killed. Some lay buried in unmarked graves in a United Nations cemetery in South Korea. Recently, the graves of four of those who died have finally been identified after painstaking years of investigation.

Michael was just a year old when his father went off to fight. He was one of several children who had been told their fathers' bodies would never be found. At last, Michael unexpectedly got the news that his father had been found. He spoke movingly, standing by the newly named graveside. "This is the closest I've been to my father in 70 years," he said, "I can't describe the emotional release; it has haunted me for years."

This is My Story

Born in the 1960s, I grew up in a happy, secure and peaceful family in a beautiful home in Surrey. My mum was a homemaker, so I still recall the smell of cooking and the warmth of the kitchen as I opened the back door after returning from school. Homemade biscuits and meals welcomed me with familiarity and security.

My dad worked very hard running his own business, and my parents did a lot of voluntary work in their spare time. We are a Christian family, so the church and its activities were a part of our lives. Several of my cousins lived within a couple of miles from us, and our grandparents too. Family gatherings, especially Christmas, were (and still are) lively and fun. Happy times, wonderful memories, and a privileged upbringing in so many ways that I only truly appreciated once I had left home and seen more of the world. I am grateful for the opportunities and blessings I have received that many do not have.

And Yet...

And yet it took until I was in my fifties, a mother of two adult children and, by then, a grandmother of four, to ask if I could call in and see Mum and Dad as I had something to ask them. A question had been gnawing away at me for some time, which I had been unwilling to face. In the familiar surroundings of my childhood home, we sat in the warm, sunny conservatory with a cup of tea and a selection of biscuits. I summed up the courage to speak. I hadn't anticipated the tears would flow as I began.

"I know it seems ridiculous to ask... but there is something I need to know... and I haven't felt able to ask you before."

My parents looked concerned as they leaned in toward me, waiting to hear me finally express my feelings. "Can I ask... I need to ask. Were you... were you disappointed when I was born?"

Having two older sisters, I am the third daughter. My brother came along two years after me. Despite the usual squabbles and fallings out as children, we all get along extremely well. We are a close-knit family, and I have never felt anything other than love from my wonderful parents. As I was growing up, I didn't think that they might be disappointed to discover I was another baby girl when I arrived that late Saturday evening in November.

I will return to my parents' response to the question later in the book. Still, when I stood back and reflected, even with all the love and security surrounding my childhood, uncertainty was in the back of my mind. Perhaps this is why I have sometimes felt inadequate, unworthy and often a people-pleaser. It may seem irrational in its context, but somehow, this unasked question had affected me without my realising it.

If that is the impact of needing to know the answer to my request, then surely others have a similar experience. I am sure there are others for whom longings, uncertainties and unspoken questions about their roots, security and family run far deeper, sharper, wider and much costlier than I've had to face.

Needing to Know

In the compelling TV series 'Long Lost Family', viewers are introduced to people who have been searching for a family member for a long time and who need help. Peter, a 58-year-old Grandad, had spent 20 years searching for his mother — to no avail. The shame and stigma of illegitimate birth, especially for a 17-year-old girl in the 1960s, meant she had no option but to give her child up for adoption.

Peter's wife knew her husband's ongoing search for his mother was crucial. "He needs to know who makes him who he is, what he is made of, and where that comes from. The mystery of who his mother is, is the one piece of him that is missing."

Michael, Frances and Peter. Three ordinary people with different stories to share about something that is missing in their lives.

In some ways, we can take sensible measures to ensure we don't miss things, such as checking the expiry date in the passport weeks before setting off for the airport, but it doesn't always work. My husband had developed an excellent system: his Six-

Step Check, for when he was about to leave each morning and again in the evening when departing the office to return home:

"1. Travel Pass ... 2. Keys ... 3. Air Pods ... 4. Phone ... 5. Security Pass ... 6. Smart Watch."

That's all well and good, but he arrived home one dark winter's evening after travelling nearly an hour from his work and discovered, to his dismay, that he had left his laptop behind. He thought his trolley case was nice and light, but he hadn't realised the vital contents were missing. He needed to do some work, so I offered to drive him back up to London to retrieve it. He was grateful but frustrated, too. When I asked him about his fail-safe system, he said he thought he had packed the computer in his bag but hadn't checked. Suffice it to say, Tony now has a seven-point check to include the laptop, or even eight – his hat – when it's wintertime!

"Missing" is a big word as it covers a wide range of situations and circumstances. Foolishly missing out one of the ingredients of a dessert is one thing, but leaving your laptop behind is another. To miss a key person or detail in your life story that is holding you back is on an entirely different level.

A Thought for Today
What is Missing?

I'm not sure why it took me until I was in my sixth decade to ask my parents that question. I wanted to know their response, but at the same time, I didn't.

- Perhaps my story will prompt you to consider whether something — or someone — is missing in your life. Is there anything that has been on your heart and mind for some time that you need to address or take the first step towards finding answers to your questions?

- What about those layers, especially those we keep hidden from view and covered up, lest anyone see into our hearts?

In Psalm 86:1, David prays: "Hear me, Lord, and answer me, for I am poor and needy."

"To be rooted is perhaps the most important and least recognised need of the human soul." — Simone Weil, a French philosopher

FRANCES MILES

Chapter 2
Looking for You

One day, I came across Coldplay's song 'Daddy' (from the album 'Everyday Life'). I recommend it.

The lyrics and tune are strikingly poignant and have deeply impacted many. It has been described as one of the most beautiful and moving songs the band has written to date. The video has reached over 26 million views on YouTube, and the comments from folk worldwide echo the child's search for her daddy and the confusion and heartbreak that he isn't there. Listening to the song and watching the official video has impacted and touched many.

So many people are searching for a parent who is missing in their life or longing for restoration in a broken relationship with a mother or father. There are those, too, who have children but, for whatever reason, are separated from them. The themes in this song (the heartfelt longing of a child, the pain and guilt of separation, but also a degree of acceptance) echo across many of our hearts and lives, which I am sure is why it has resonated with countless people.

I want to introduce you to six individuals in this chapter:

- A little boy I met briefly at a football match.
- A young girl I encountered on the underground.
- The former British Paralympic swimmer, Ellie Simmonds.
- Jenna was searching for a dad she had never met.
- And finally, the parents of a young lad born over 2,000 years ago in Bethlehem, Judea, whose name was Jesus.

The theme of separation and searching connects their stories.

"I Think I've Lost My Daddy."

Good Friday, 2013. As I have already mentioned, my husband is a Methodist Minister, so this holy day is busy for our household. Once the church services were over and the hot cross buns eaten, we hastily made our way to a football ground in North London to watch our son, on his twentieth birthday, make his debut for a team in goal.

A small boy and his dad sat next to us during the match. Toward the end of half-time, the dad went to get food and told his son to remain in his seat. The first I knew about it was a tap on my arm. I turned to see the child with a curled lip, about to cry. "Excuse me, I think I've lost my Daddy," he said. He had been looking all around him, but his father, who had gone to join a queue, had been out of sight for quite a while. I put my arm around his shoulders and tried to spot a match steward to help when his dad reappeared with a tray of drinks, burgers and fries. A daddy reunited with his son — albeit after a brief interlude — was a great relief for us all.

A short while later, I checked on him and was sorry to see that my young friend was still a bit upset. "I've got my little boy here today, too. Shall I show you where he is?" I asked. "There he is!" I pointed to my son, the 6' 2" player wearing goalie gloves on the pitch and playing for his team right before us. The young lad smiled, and all was well.

Sliding Doors

The loss of or a complete separation from a father or mother figure impacts so many of us — at different stages of our lives and circumstances. It can be for just a moment, like the young child whose mother was trapped inside an underground train by the closing doors while her daughter had already alighted onto the platform with others in their group. The little girl started to scream uncontrollably in shock at the realisation of the sudden separation of her mum still on the train. Standing next to her, I instinctively tried to soothe and reassure her, but she was inconsolable. Thankfully, the train wasn't going anywhere because of a signalling problem. A conductor soon came along the platform and managed to open the doors to release the mum. Mercifully, the situation lasted less than a few minutes, but seeing a distressed child was nonetheless painful.

"The Most Amazing Feeling"

Some people who were adopted at a very young age may have questions that they wish to have answered. Ellie Simmonds, the multiple gold-medal-winning British Paralympian and now sports presenter, won her first two gold medals in swimming when she was 13. In 2023, she made a documentary called 'Finding My Secret Family' (ITVX) about her life as an adopted daughter and the journey she took to meet her birth mother.

Ellie grew up with wonderful parents and siblings; she always knew she was adopted, but after retiring from sport, she felt it was time to connect with her identity and background. Ellie confessed that the process was an emotional rollercoaster, especially leading up to meeting her birth mother for the first time since she was just a few days old.

"The first moment of meeting her, we just embraced. It was the most amazing feeling when you meet someone who looks like you, with the same personality." For Ellie, it was the opportunity to put the missing pieces of the puzzle together and find the answers to the questions she had longed to ask.

"I Really Want to Know Where I Come From."

During an episode of 'Long Lost Family' (ITVX, 2024), a lady called Jenna travelled to Oxford for the first time since her birth. She had been born 40 years earlier via donor conception after her parents had struggled with infertility. In line with the law at the time, Jenna's mother had not been given any details about the donor in terms of physical characteristics, age, status, etc. After four decades of no information, Jenna was desperate for some answers. She wondered whether she had any half-siblings.

Jenna needed to go to the place that was significant to her. She would walk around, wondering if the people passing her might be a sibling, perhaps even her biological dad. "I would just like to know, is there someone else out there that is half of me? I really want to know where I come from." Sadly, Jenna could not trace the biological father, but she discovered a half-sister during the search. Meeting her and finding many common personality traits and interests between them brought joy and some closure to her long quest for answers.

"... He Was the Son, So It Was Thought of Joseph..."

Biblical accounts and other reliable sources document the birth of a historical Jesus in a little town called Bethlehem. What is more unusual is His family situation, and His genealogy is open to question. In the first chapter of the gospel of Luke, the young virgin Mary is unexpectedly visited by an angel and told that she will bear God's Son.

Joseph, to whom Mary is betrothed, does the right thing and undertakes to support and look after her. I wonder how hard that was for him. The biblical accounts tell us very little about what happened beyond that time, in those years when Jesus was growing up. However, thanks to the writer Luke, we can read an account of an essential stage in his development.

Jesus, at 12 years old, is on the verge of adulthood, according to Jewish tradition. Following a regular annual visit to the Temple in Jerusalem, his parents go on ahead, not realising their Son is still in the Temple. After an anxious search, they find Him sitting amongst the teachers of the law and engaging in debate with them. Like all parents who lose their child unintentionally, there must have been panic, stress and worry. Notice the exasperated Mary and her Son's response in Luke 2:48, '"Son, why have you treated us like this? Your father and I have been anxiously searching for You." "Why were you searching for Me?" He asked. "Didn't you know I had to be in My Father's house?"'

At this age, Jesus knew who His real Father was; He was sure and confident of His destiny and was growing in wisdom and stature — a leader in the making! It can't have been easy for the family during those years, but Luke tells us that afterwards, Jesus "went down to Nazareth with them and was obedient to them." The next time we see Him, Luke records: "...Jesus Himself was about thirty years old when He began His ministry. He was the Son, so it was thought of Joseph..." (Luke 3:23)

Jesus had the most unique start in life, with a mother who had become "with child" before she was married, and a stepfather. Not long after His birth, the family was forced to become refugees to flee a tyrant leader. I'm sure a TV documentary team would have loved to have interviewed all the different characters of this narrative and gotten their perspectives on it — as well as the wider family members and any local people who might have enjoyed a bit of gossip about them.

The little boy at the football match, the young girl from the tube train, Ellie and Jenna, and Mary and Joseph were all on their journeys of searching for what was missing. Even with my limited knowledge, I know that many people who do not grow up with their biological parents are brought up in very loving and supportive households.

I believe it is essential to respect and love those families that are blended through means other than biology. Ellie didn't undertake her search for her biological mother because she was unhappy in her adopted family but because she had come to a point in her life when she wanted answers about her own identity. I haven't been directly impacted by adoption, so I cannot speak from my own experience. However, I do know people who are adopted or who have been adoptive parents themselves.

Around 3,000 children are adopted in England each year. The current practice is to allow letters to be exchanged between birth families and their children, usually twice a year. A review of the adoption process was carried out in 2024, and the working group responsible for the report highlighted the need for a more open process that includes consideration of face-to-face contact with birth families. Of course, any change impacts not only the birth parents and the child but also the wider extended family. Navigating a path through this complex situation can be challenging, but placing a child's best interests at the centre must surely be the most important priority.

A Thought for Today
Looking for Someone

Describing the different people and their situations in this chapter may cause us to think about what or who is missing from our lives. These gaps could be aspects of connection, purpose or understanding that we feel are lacking or incomplete.

- How can we find answers to the questions that help us begin to complete the picture? What and who are we looking for?

- Can the Bible give us some answers? It can, and as we read on, hopefully, you will agree it does.

Chapter 3
"You Are My Son..."

"And a voice came from heaven: 'You are my Son, whom I love; with You I am well pleased'".

(Mark 1:11)

Finding Out Who You Are

"A people without the knowledge of their history, origin and culture is like a tree without roots." — Marcus Garvey

I have enjoyed learning about my family tree, thanks to my parents and uncle's research. As mentioned, I was raised in a Christian home, and discovering something about my family's history is fascinating and genuinely humbling.

I have come across stories of faith and service from my ancestors. My great-great-grandfather on my father's side was an ardent Wesleyan preacher and evangelist in the mid-1800s. Edmund would travel for miles to preach the Gospel in eastern England. He felt a desire to love and serve God at the age of nine and was in a leadership position in church at just 19. On my mother's side is Alfred, my great-grandfather. He gave his life to God at the age of ten, under the ministry of his mother, Emily. In 1890, at just 17, Alfred was sent to Buenos Aires to support a small pioneer team. An extraordinary life of service and worldwide ministry began with the Salvation Army, which continued through subsequent generations.

Edmund and Alfred were influenced by their parents, who passed on their active Christian faith to their families. The wonderful phrase "standing on the shoulders of giants" comes to mind. I am profoundly grateful and humbled for the legacy I have inherited.

One of the main reasons I wrote this book is that understanding who we are is at the heart of being human. I have been looking particularly at why discovering our roots can be crucial to appreciating our identity. Understanding our connections with others and our past can help put some pieces together of who we are.

An Unfinished Jigsaw

A radio programme described the remarkable story of two baby girls born at the same hospital on the same day in 1967.[1] Somehow, the girls were mistakenly swapped in the nursery. Without realising it, the mums took the wrong babies home and brought them up as their own. This wasn't uncovered until over fifty years later. A DNA kit was used by a family member who had been given it as a gift one Christmas. They left the kit on the shelf unopened for some time and then one day decided to give it a go. A series of events began to unfold.

Consequences

Once the truth had been confirmed, the ripple effect of what that meant for both families and the psychological impact, especially on the mothers and daughters, was immense. For one of the daughters, however, discovering the truth helped put those pieces of the jigsaw together that didn't make sense to her growing up. "I always felt like an outsider in my family," she said. "Now, this has answered the questions in my life."

As I pondered stories like these, I realised that the Bible not only contains the key to making sense of life's big questions but also reveals the significance of a special event in Jesus' life.

Jesus and John and the Important Event

The gospel writers pick up the story of Jesus when He was thirty years old. He was about to take on a new, significant, life-changing role. Leaving His family and work behind, we read the following:

"At that time, Jesus came from Nazareth in Galilee and was baptised by John in the Jordan. Just as Jesus was coming up out of the water, He saw heaven being torn open and the Spirit descending on Him like a dove. And a voice came from heaven: 'You are my Son, whom I love; with You I am well pleased'" (Mark 1:9–11).

It can be challenging to comprehend the Christian belief that Jesus was human but also divine. Still, here, in this moment, the three persons of the Trinity were present: Father, Son and Holy Spirit. Luke records the event as "the Holy Spirit descended on Him in bodily form like a dove" (Luke 3:22). The striking image of "heaven being torn open" in Mark 1 tells the reader that something significant is happening. Jesus was about to begin His ministry and reveal the truth in word and deed. This was a critical moment.

It was at this historic juncture God the Father spoke these words to His son Jesus:

- "You are my son". God is saying to Jesus: "You belong to me". Rooted.
- "Whom I love". The Father's heart is revealed to His son. Loved.
- "With you, I am well pleased." God is proud of Jesus. Affirmed.

Jesus, who understood who He was and what He had to do by the age of twelve, nonetheless received confirmation at this crucial time.

Jesus, the One with the unconventional parentage, was being affirmed by His Heavenly Father. You are Mine! This is where You belong.

Jesus, no doubt loved by His earthly parents, heard His Heavenly Parent declare His love for Him.

Jesus, a carpenter until now, had not become a full-time preacher or leader of His ragamuffin band of disciples. As far as it is recorded, He had not yet taught truths through parables, turned water into wine, calmed a storm on a lake, miraculously provided lunch for 5,000 or taught His followers how to pray.

Yet God knew His Son; He knew He was ready. God saw Him, and God recognised His worth.

Calvin Miller wrote the profoundly beautiful and hugely impactful book 'The Singer'.[2] I highly recommend it. It is written in allegorical form, in the style of CS Lewis or JRR Tolkien. The main character knows his calling – to be "the singer" and sing the "song", but for now, he is still a tradesman. The music resonating in his soul is getting louder, though, so he makes his way to the river and finds John.

It is when the River Singer (John the Baptist) and the Tradesman (Jesus the Carpenter) are in the water, they both hear the music begin and then a voice from above declaring:

"Tradesman! You are the Troubadour! Go now and sing!"

The Tradesman has received the confirmation He needed; now, He will fulfil His destiny as the Singer.

And so it is with Jesus. But first, He had to encounter a real challenge. Immediately following His baptism, the gospel writers describe Jesus going to a wilderness for 40 days, where He didn't eat or drink.

After this time, Jesus is visited by Satan, who takes the opportunity to exploit His hunger, thirst and exhaustion and to question who He is.

Jesus hears another voice, but this time, it is to tear down and challenge what He had just heard at His baptism: "If You are the Son of God..."

Why not try reading this question aloud and emphasise the different words each time you say it:

"IF you are the Son of God..."

If YOU are the Son of God..."

If you ARE the Son of God..."

If you are THE Son of God..."

If you are the SON of God..."

If you are the Son OF GOD..."

It is remarkable that by focusing on separate words, each brings a subtly different meaning to the fore. How clever and manipulating that question must have been, so much more so when the hearer is in a state of vulnerability, depletion and weakness!

This reminds me of what we read in Genesis at the beginning of the Bible. God had spoken to Adam, and he was free to eat from any tree in the garden except one: the tree of the knowledge of good and evil. Later, while Eve is alone, Satan, in the form of a snake, sows a seed of doubt into her mind: "Did God really say...?"

Suppose Jesus had not previously received words of confirmation and love. Would He have been able to withstand the Devil's questioning? The chief manipulator enticed Jesus to mistrust what He had heard from His Father and tempted Him to misuse His power. What a different outcome there would have been if Jesus had crumbled in the face of extreme pressure.

What Children Want to Hear

Hearing our parents speak to us can be life-enhancing, especially at difficult times. Gaby Eirew is a well-being specialist, counsellor and creator of the app "RecordMeNow".[3] She supports and encourages people to live well and leave messages for their loved ones, especially their children. Over five years, Eirew interviewed more than 100 people in Canada and the UK who had lost one or both parents as children. She asked people who had recently been bereaved what they wished they could have asked their parents before they died. "The single most important thing that people said they wanted to hear was that their parents were proud of them, that they loved them and to hear them say that with their name," Gaby says. "So often people were told that their mum or dad loved them so much, but they needed and wanted to hear it."

Children want to hear from their parents precisely what God said to Jesus at the start of His new and most important work. God the Father blessed Jesus for His ministry ahead, telling Him that He belonged to Him.

A Thought for Today
Belonging to God

For Jesus, hearing the words "You are My Son" from the heavens must have been so impactful. We might not have our parents around to hear them affirm us as their children. It might be that our childhood was not supportive or a secure enough anchor as we grew up. The Bible describes God as our Heavenly Father who cares deeply for us.

- Why not read Psalm 23? It describes the Lord as our Shepherd, and our belonging to Him: "He leads me beside quiet waters, He refreshes my soul... surely Your goodness and love will follow me all the days of my life, and I will dwell in the house of the Lord forever."

- Maybe today is a good opportunity to let that truth sink into our hearts and minds and give us peace.

What did it mean for Jesus to hear out loud that He was loved, and how did that impact His interactions with others and the parables He told? We will explore that in the next chapter, but before we continue, I want to say something about our language when describing God.

A Little Note

I don't believe God is physically male or female. He is above all of that. God is God, and I think He holds everything good and perfect about motherhood and fatherhood together in the persons of the Trinity — Father, Son and Holy Spirit. I was privileged to be given an opportunity to think about this when I was a young adult. In the late 1980s, I attended a weekend retreat by Rosemary Wakelin. She taught that it is the Jewish and Christian belief that we are all made in God's image: God who is the "Alpha and Omega… the Beginning and the End" (Revelation 22:13).

The teaching greatly impacted me. In a sermon (published on "collegeofpreachers.co.uk" in November 2022), Rosemary Wakelin further explained her reasoning about the character of God as described in the Bible. She wrote: "We readily recognise the Alpha — the initiator, the powerful, the One in control. But what about the Omega? … My reading of the gospels shows me a Jesus who refused to accept the leadership of a resistance army, who redefined kingship — nothing to do with wealth, palaces, privilege, but caring and serving; who told Peter to put away his sword when Peter tried to defend Him. Jesus had amazing Alpha powers of leadership, crowd control, preaching, charisma, but never compelled or overpowered. He made space for people, accepted them as they were, enabled them to become what they were made to be. He had Alpha and Omega in balance."

I have benefitted from pondering the Alpha and Omega perspectives. For this book, I use the term "Father" because Jesus did when He talked about God and in His prayers.

FRANCES MILES

Chapter 4
"...Whom I Love"

"And a voice came from heaven: 'You are My Son, whom I love; with You I am well pleased'"

(Mark 1:11).

I am sure you don't need reminding of the first line of The Beatles' 1967 hit, 'All You Need is Love'. Love is a powerful word used thousands of times in songs, books, films and TV shows. There were several words for love in the biblical Greek language, covering different aspects or perspectives. "Agape" is the highest form of love — God's love for a person and a person's love for God. Then there are words for intimate love, affectionate love between friends (also known as "brotherly love"), family love and self-love.

God the Father told His Son that He loved Him at His moment of baptism and at a crucial time in His life.

David Mathis writes: "The Father also says, "You are my beloved Son."[4] Few words in all the world carry such power as a father's declaration of love for his son. Few words are as profound in forming and securing the bonds that hold society together. And few words cause as much harm and instability when they go unexpressed, or when a father gives his son the impression of contempt. Or perhaps worse: apathy."

Lost and Found Again

The "Prodigal" phrase is often quoted. It comes from one of the best-known stories (or parables) that Jesus told, describing a father with two sons. One remains faithfully at home working for the family business, while the other boy decides to go his own way and do his own thing. He leaves home, taking his share of his father's inheritance and travels to a distant land.

The story continues, and this younger brother squanders his money. As that disappears, so do his new friends and, with them, any security, comfort, or food. With the land in the grip of famine, he can only find a job feeding pigs in a landowner's fields.

We're told that the young man came to his senses and realised his father's servants had a much better life than he did. So, he heads back towards home, a changed man from his outward journey, rehearsing what to tell his father that he has made a mess of his life. He is a sinner. He is not worthy to be called a son, but would he please make him a hired servant? Of course, he has no idea whether his father or older brother will accept him.

While He Was Still A Long Way Off

The father has been waiting all this time, waiting and longing for his boy to return. The boy who rejected his love and lifestyle rebelled, tried to do things his way and was left bankrupt.

While he is still a long way off, the father sees him. He sees the boy he loves. The Bible says he was filled with compassion for him and came running out to him, throwing his arms around him and kissing him.

This powerful story of redemption, fatherly love and forgiveness is told by someone brought up by a mother and an adopted father who knew he also had a heavenly, perfect Father. God spoke words over Him at a significant time in His life. He doesn't have children, and so what Jesus describes in the story is, I would surmise, coming from the example of His earthly dad's love and His Heavenly Father. Still, more importantly, the love of God that Jesus knew was there not just for Him alone but for those who were lost: the sinners — you and me. Jesus, through His words and later through His death on the cross, offers reconciliation and hope.

Unspoken Love

Charlie is a friend of ours. He told me this story about his son and was happy for me to share it here:

"Joe is autistic and, for a long time, wasn't overly affectionate, which has been a particularly hard adjustment as I love a hug. We regularly take him swimming as it's one of his favourite things to do, and we enjoy it as a family. After one session, we sat on a sofa in the café, drinking hot chocolate, and Joe, feeling very satisfied and happy, sidled up to me, put his head on my chest and hugged me. It was one of the best moments of my life, just sitting there feeling close and enjoying a hug together. It made me realise how God longs for us to hug and get close to Him and allow Him to comfort us under His wing."

There are different ways we can express love. I confess that I don't always get it right. That story Jesus told about the waiting and running father always touches me whenever I think about it. What was Jesus trying to say to His hearers in this story? If God loves me — and I turn to Him in faith and repentance — then am I loved by the same Heavenly Father who declared His love for His Son at His baptism? For me, that is truly mind-blowing!

In his book, 'The Ragamuffin Gospel', Brennan Manning describes how prayer to God should be trusting in the Father's delight that we spend time with Him. He quotes the Trappist Monk, Basil Pennington: "A father is delighted when his little one, leaving off his toys and friends, runs to him and climbs into his arms ... essentially the child is choosing to be with his father, confident of the love, the care, the security that is his in those arms."

The child doesn't have to earn his father's love, just as we cannot do anything to earn God's love for us. There is a verse in the Bible which says, "See what great love the Father has lavished on us, that we should be called children of God! And that is what we are!" (1 John 3:1)

John Wesley was an English cleric, theologian, and evangelist in the eighteenth century who led a revival movement within the Church of England, which eventually became known as "Methodism". John, his brother Charles, and others in that movement were nicknamed "Methodists" because they were so methodical in their spirituality and practices. John's belief and trust in a God of love and mercy gave him a burning desire to tell others about it. It compelled him to share the Gospel with anyone who would listen in the market squares of towns and villages. He preached to people working in fields and factories, as well as coal miners and commoners. John took the message to those who, perhaps ordinarily, wouldn't be able to attend church so that they could nonetheless hear that God loved them. It is said that Wesley delivered 40,000 sermons during his lifetime and rode a quarter of a million miles on horseback! He wanted people to hear, understand and accept the good news that Jesus died on the cross for their sins, receive forgiveness and transform their lives in response for the sake of others.

Karl Barth (1886–1986) was a renowned and respected Swiss theologian. It is believed that during the Q&A session after a lecture at the University of Chicago in 1962, a student asked Barth if he could summarise his whole life's work in theology in a sentence. Barth replied: "Yes, I can. In the words of a song I learned at my mother's knee: 'Jesus loves me, this I know, for the Bible tells me so.'"

A Thought for Today
"...Whom I Love."

I was chatting with a man whose son had not been in touch with him for a long time. Even though he had contacted his son, the young man still hadn't returned his calls or messages. Despite this, he continues to love him and says, "My door is always open to him... he is my prodigal."

- Who are the prodigals in my life? If I believe God loves even me and can grant me forgiveness, can I extend an offer of love and forgiveness to them, or is it too much to bear?

- Have I acted like a prodigal — by running away from someone or hiding from a problematic situation? Even though it isn't always easy to look beyond ourselves when going through a difficult period, the Bible appeals to us to do just that and to focus on the One who is greater than us or our problems. He can help us.

In Psalm 105, the writer extols the virtues of giving praise to God and remembering His goodness to us: "Look to the Lord and His strength; seek His face always."

The Prodigal Son: Story In Full

Here is Jesus' story of the lost son, taken directly from the Bible. You might want to read it out loud or quietly to yourself. Take your time. If this passage is familiar, ask the Lord for fresh insight into its meaning today.

"Jesus continued: 'There was a man who had two sons. The younger one said to his father, 'Father, give me my share of the estate.' So he divided his property between them.

'Not long after that, the younger son got together all he had, set off for a distant country and there squandered his wealth in wild living. After he had spent everything, there was a severe famine in that whole country, and he began to be in need. So he went and hired himself out to a citizen of that country, who sent him to his fields to feed pigs. He longed to fill his stomach with the pods that the pigs were eating, but no one gave him anything.

'When he came to his senses, he said, 'How many of my father's hired servants have food to spare, and here I am starving to death! I will set out and go back to my father and say to him: 'Father, I have sinned against heaven and against you. I am no longer worthy to be called your son; make me like one of your hired servants.' So he got up and went to his father.

'But while he was still a long way off, his father saw him and was filled with compassion for him; he ran to his son, threw his arms around him and kissed him.

The son said to him, 'Father, I have sinned against heaven and against you. I am no longer worthy to be called your son.' But the father said to his servants, 'Quick! Bring the best robe and put it on him. Put a ring on his finger and sandals on his feet. Bring the fattened calf and kill it. Let's have a feast and celebrate. For this son of mine was dead and is alive again; he was lost and is found.' So they began to celebrate.

'Meanwhile, the older son was in the field. When he came near the house, he heard music and dancing. So he called one of the servants and asked him what was going on. 'Your brother has come,' he replied, 'And your father has killed the fattened calf because he has him back safe and sound.' The older brother became angry and refused to go in. So his father went out and pleaded with him. But he answered his father, 'Look! All these years I've been slaving for you and never disobeyed your orders. Yet you never gave me even a young goat so I could celebrate with my friends. But when this son of yours who has squandered your property with prostitutes comes home, you kill the fattened calf for him!' 'My son,' the father said, 'You are always with me, and everything I have is yours. But we had to celebrate and be glad, because this brother of yours was dead and is alive again; he was lost and is found.'"

- If this passage is familiar to you, what struck you afresh as you reread it today? Has it raised questions in your mind related to your own experience?

We will shortly move on to the third declaration in God the Father's words to Jesus ("With you, I am well pleased"). But let us continue to think about real life and the challenges it presents.

Chapter 5
Love In An Imperfect World

When our five-year-old son misbehaved one afternoon, he was sent to his room. After a short time, he was allowed downstairs again. Jonathan descended with heavy feet and a stern look on his face. Staring straight at my husband, he said, "I'm really cross with you, Dad, but I still love you." His words took us both by surprise. We didn't expect him to tell his dad he loved him! Moreover, a five-year-old had just pinched the line his father was about to deliver.

Small Mirrors

How we are loved as children and young people can significantly impact us, even into adulthood. A girl was told by her stepmother that she was ugly, useless and would never achieve anything in life. Growing up, she could only bear to look in a small bathroom mirror to clean her teeth. When she was older, she became a Christian and bought her first full-length mirror. She then knew and believed God utterly loved her, and that impacted her life and changed her perspective from hating herself and her reflection to knowing she was worthy of love.

Doing the Best We Can In An Imperfect World

Being a parent or caregiver is hard enough. Still, it can be even more challenging if we put ourselves under too much pressure to get everything right. Through the years of raising our children, I often felt all the shades of guilt, joy, pride and worry — mixed up with overwhelming love — sometimes in the wee small hours when I couldn't sleep, with so many thoughts running around my head:

- "I'm relieved that the situation has resolved itself. She handled that so well. But I am worried about what she said to me today."

- "I'm dreading having to address that with him tomorrow."

- "How do I ask her teacher if she needs more support?"

- "Argh! I just remembered that I forgot to change the dates of the children's dentist appointments."

- "Did his friend say he could come to tea tomorrow, or was it Thursday...?"

- "I should have said I was sorry for how I spoke to my son today."

- "Actually, I should apologise to my husband, too."

- "Where did I put that authorisation slip that needs to be returned to school?"

- "Why isn't she back home yet? Where is she? Oh, Lord, please keep her safe."

Good Enough?

How do I ever get a sense of peace over whether I am doing, or have done, a "good enough" job as a parent or caregiver? Feeling guilty is a common human emotion that can take over our lives and squash us if we are not careful. I look again to that significant event with Jesus in the River Jordan, being baptised by John. The Father speaks words to Jesus to reassure Him of who He is, that He loves Him, and that He has seen and affirmed Him, even though Jesus had not at that stage begun what He was sent to earth to do.

When it is put like that, I may have a chance. An imperfect parent, yes, of course, yet can I do even a tiny measure of those three things with my children? And my grandkids? And my nieces and nephews, and great nieces and nephews? My godchildren? I think when children are small, they don't see our human frailties, but when they get older, their experience expands, and there must come a time when perhaps reality sets in.

I have learned that this is especially true for boys and their dads. It has been said that a child's father is a hero up to the age of ten, but if something happens around that age, it can change that perception.

A friend, whom I shall call Ruth, described when she went to a parent's evening to see the teacher and get a report on her then 10-year-old son Ryan. Her husband Peter couldn't be there, but she was interested in looking at the work displayed on Ryan's desk. Ruth's son's handwriting on a piece of paper stopped her short and has remained etched in her memory: "I saved up my pocket money to buy something I really wanted and had enough money, but Dad said 'no' — as always." Ryan's father had been raised in a very authoritarian home; his father had been a military colonel, and Peter was, in turn, the same with his sons. Here, in that piece of writing, young Ryan was coming to terms with the disappointment and sadness he had been feeling and expressed it with such pathos.

Then there is Jeffrey, who had several issues and needs which appeared to stem from some trauma he had experienced growing up. He was estranged from his family and especially missed his dad, so much so that he had been buying a gift for him every birthday. The presents were stacked up in the corner of his room, ready to be given should Jeffrey ever have the opportunity to be reunited with him.

The nineteenth-century poet Henry Longfellow wrote, "Every man has his secret sorrows which the world knows not, and oftentimes we call a man cold when he is only sad." Considering this hugely important subject of love, I am conscious of those who have had tough starts in life, who have not truly experienced love from parents, or who are struggling to love their own family. It is easy to get overwhelmed by our failings or to think we don't deserve to love or to be loved.

Thinking back to the story of the lady with just one small mirror in her house: How small are the physical and symbolic mirrors in our homes and hearts? Why do we consider ourselves so unworthy not to accept who we are? I want to emulate the wonder of my 16-month-old granddaughter, who discovered that when she smiled, the little person in the large mirror in front of her did, too, and when she moved, so did the other girl. This discovery made her laugh and prompted her grandmother to be thankful for childlike curiosity and confidence and, above all, finding joy in the simple things.

A Thought for Today
Swopping It Out

Love between fallible people in an imperfect world is not easy. Still, it is worth trying, even if we feel, at times, unlovable. Negative words or actions can affect our well-being, whether from others, ourselves, or even projected onto others. Here's an exercise to try:

- Feeling unloved or worthless? Replace with an understanding that you are precious.

- Handling cynicism? Replace with a word or two of kindness.

- Tempted to use sarcasm? Replace with honest feedback and a different mindset.

- Does our heart seem hardened, and our fists clenched? How about we seek to be vulnerable enough to soften our hearts and open our hands?

- Feeling unseen and unnoticed? Well, let's look at that one as you continue to read!

"When someone loves you, the way they say your name is different. You just know that your name is safe in their mouth," Billy, age four, said.

We return to God the Father's interaction at Jesus' baptism and to the final words He declared: "With You, I am well pleased.

FRANCES MILES

Chapter 6
"With You I Am Well-Pleased"

"And a voice came from heaven: 'You are My Son, whom I love; with You I am well pleased'" (Mark 1:11).

A teacher noticed a girl's talent at school: "You are a singer."

The pupil didn't believe it but was again told, "You are a singer!" Those words empowered the young lady, and in time, she became a member of the prestigious D'oly Carte Opera.

The converse happened to me once upon a time. As a teenager, I was a member of a young people's music group and loved participating. One day, we were practising harmonies, and a fellow member of the choir told me he thought I couldn't sing in tune. That knocked my confidence then, and in fact, it has stayed with me, making me feel a bit cautious and self-conscious when I'm singing in a choir or informal group. I still enjoy it, though, and playing music or singing can benefit a person's well-being and sense of community. I am sharing this story because it reminds me to be aware of the impact of my actions and words on others, however small or insignificant they may seem at the time. At a crucial moment, Jesus heard His Heavenly Father use words to validate Him — before He had even begun His ministry.

I have already noted that Joseph was known as Jesus' adopted dad. Mary is a prominent character in school and church nativity plays, and so is the angel, but Joseph is more of an "OK yeah... I'll just be the support act." We can understand that Joseph is somewhat on the sidelines. Just an ordinary man, just a carpenter. Just a concerned husband-to-be, an uncertain father-to-be, and then a dad to this unique child. So, nothing more than that. Or was he? Jesus told parables about fathers, so He must have been influenced by him. Joseph's skill as a carpenter would have impacted the young boy. Jesus learned to work with wood; how profound when He was nailed to a wooden cross to die.

Jesus was raised in a family by a man of faith who stood by his wife when the world would have looked upon her with shame and accusation. His strength of character and belief in God were evident. And then, of course, there was His faithful, humble, insightful and courageous mother. What a family to be born into! God was undoubtedly well-pleased with Jesus, not just because of His calling but also as a result of Mary and Joseph's parenting and influence.

Let no one tell you you're unimportant or just a person on the sidelines, in other people's shadows. You are noticed. God sees you. You, too, can notice others and validate who they are. You may recall being noticed as a child for something good or helpful you did or said. Receiving that "specific praise" from a parent, sibling, or peer group can be impactful.

Being Noticed in a Crowd

Have you ever been in a crowd and felt unseen? My son and I attended a Carling Cup football final at Wembley one year. A mere 88,000 others were there that day, including us! TV cameras were around, interviews were taking place before the match started, and excitement was building. Who got interviewed or filmed? Not us, the ordinary ones, just part of the large group. Instead, the people who stood out in the crowd — those dressed up in funny costumes or with striking face paints, the ones with wigs to support their team colour, and the cute little children jumping up and down and singing songs. The rest of us were somewhat ignored! Maybe you know how it feels when you are often overlooked and excluded from the "in-crowd".

The Named and the Unnamed

In the Bible, we read of an occasion when Jesus was in a great crowd. Someone needed to be noticed. His name was Jairus, an important religious man. He pushed himself through the throng right up in front of Jesus. He threw himself at Jesus' feet and pleaded for Him to come to the house and heal his very sick 12-year-old daughter.

In the gospel accounts, there are many stories of Jesus encountering people — at their point of need and when they were in the right place and at the right time (e.g., the boy who offered his picnic lunch of a few loaves and fish). But we are also told of the occasions when Jesus notices the unnoticed. Perhaps you agree that sometimes we might feel unnoticed, especially if we are always "doing" for others.

While Jesus is heading to Jairus' house, someone else is mentioned; someone unnoticed by the crowd, a very sick lady. We are not told her name, but we learn that she had been suffering from continuous bleeding for 12 years. No doctor could help her, and she was no doubt shunned by her family, friends and local community because of being considered permanently unclean. This poor woman we don't know her name, age, or any other details about her — is stuck in this heaving crowd. And yet, she believes that Jesus can heal her. Rather than pushing through the crowd and coming face to face with the Healer, this lady creeps up behind Him and touches the edges of His cloak. Immediately, her bleeding ceases.

If you have been in a crushing crowd (and as a football fan who enjoys attending matches to watch my team, I frequently am), you will know what pushing and shoving goes on. Yet Jesus is aware that someone has touched His cloak and won't be put off by the disciples pointing out the obvious fact that, of course, He had been touched there was a whole crowd pressing in on Him!

But Jesus knew, and He sought out the woman in the crowd. She then did the same as Jairus but approached Jesus without boldness. Instead, trembling in fear, she fell at His feet. The healing transformed that woman's life physically, emotionally, socially and spiritually.

There is another occasion when Jesus notices someone, so the gospel writer Luke tells us. This time, we meet Zacchaeus, a wealthy tax collector and a hugely unpopular man. He was undoubtedly like the sick woman, rather shunned in his locality. Well, Zacchaeus hears that Jesus is passing through his hometown of Jericho. He isn't very tall, so Zacchaeus climbs a sycamore tree to peer out to see Jesus as He enters the town. It was probably a good place to look from but not be seen! Jesus, however, comes straight over. He spots Zaccheaus and invites him to come down from his hiding place. Jesus spends time with him at his home, and the outcome is positive.

Who are you most like in these stories?

- You might be a Jairus figure: full of confidence, who can boldly come to Jesus in prayer, fall at His feet, and tell Him your fears, problems and needs, knowing He can see and hear you.

- Perhaps you feel like the unnamed woman in the story: Exhausted by life, lost in the crowd, and needing Jesus' healing touch just as much as anyone else. You are trying to reach out for the hem of His cloak.

- Or, maybe you identify most with Zacchaeus because you want to know more about Jesus but are worried about what He will think of you or say to you if He sees you for who you are.

Despite the crowds, Jesus saw Jairus and his unnamed daughter. He also noticed Zacchaeus and the nameless, sick woman and dealt with them as individuals. Jesus does the same with us. He sees you and me for who we are, our good side, and the things we would rather keep hidden. He offers love and forgiveness to each one of us.

Noticing and Acknowledging

Noticing and acknowledging are essential in everyday life, including work relationships between a manager and an employee, a CEO and the security staff, a doctor and a patient, or a teacher and pupil.

I once overheard part of a conversation on a train. It was between two middle-aged men discussing their business and various current matters. Responding to a question about a particular staff member, one replied very casually to the other: "Yeah, he reports to me on an org chart somewhere." I found that to be rather curious and off-hand. Perhaps it was an attempt by the businessman to impress his companion, but it bothered me. Of course, I don't know the setup or whether an extensive department was being discussed. Still, it made me ponder the senior executive's approach to management and whether he took time to notice individuals under his authority and their contributions to the company.

In addition to our interactions across several settings, noticing and acknowledging each other is even more vital in the family sphere and its various relationship dynamics, especially in the home.

Many of us don't like mornings and find it hard to respond when the alarm goes off. One morning, a man was next to me on the bus as I was going to the train station to get to work. He made three phone calls in quick succession. I guessed he was a dad phoning his son or daughter:

7:16 am: "It's time to get up," he whispered loudly.

7:19 am — a little more urgently: "It's time to get up!"

7:21 am — with more urgency and some irritation: "It's time to get up... But you don't sound like you're up... You sound horizontal... OK, let me hear water so I know you're up."

The man put the phone away for the last time. I pictured a teenager receiving those calls, not wanting to respond, annoyed at their dad for phoning three times, and wishing they could remain horizontal with the duvet's warmth for comfort and to go back to sleep. But just maybe they were secretly pleased that someone was thinking of them, who believed in them and cared enough to make those calls, urging them to get going and not miss out on the day's opportunities.

It has been said that when we are affirmed and validated by others, we feel empowered to reach our goals and strive for excellence. I believe God's spoken words provide a blueprint for our feelings of self-worth, security and fulfilment, and this is what hit me when I read the passage about Jesus' baptism (and later the Transfiguration). I had spent years gathering stories of people who had needed their parents' validation or were searching for love, safety and security. So many people grow up with low self-esteem and live with uncertainty about their identity. But these words spoken by the Heavenly Father are what any of us can read, listen to and benefit from, whatever our earthly circumstances.

Let's remind ourselves: Jesus heard this deeply personal message from Heaven: "You are My Son, whom I love; with You, I am well-pleased."

Let that sink in and be a blessing to you.

A Thought for Today
Seeing Others and Showing You Care

The fantastic charity I used to work for, Stewardship,[5] ran a successful Lent campaign for many years. The idea was that instead of giving something up during that period, people were encouraged to participate in a daily act of kindness that would benefit someone else. The suggestions were varied and sometimes challenging. One that I particularly remember was to write a note along the lines of: "You are unique, and you are loved." I came across one of these myself. It was left on the mirror of the ladies' cloakroom at a train station. Even though I knew about the campaign, reading those affirming words was a nice surprise.

- I know a dad who sometimes writes messages for his children when packing their school lunch boxes. It might contain a joke, an interesting fact, a quotation, or a simple: "I love you, and I am thinking about you." This is a fantastic idea, especially in a family with more than one child. It can help reinforce someone's sense of worth and identity.

- Even for the adults in our lives, writing and hiding a note for a loved one or a special friend to discover when they unexpectedly open a drawer or move a cushion might be really appreciated.

- Why not consider a small act of kindness for a stranger? Leaving your pound coin in a shopping trolley could make someone else's day!

Chapter 7
Fathers and Sons

"It is a wise father that knows his own child."
William Shakespeare

Steve Biddulph is a respected Australian psychologist and author, who has written several books about parenting, particularly the role of fathers. He speaks with men about their own fathers and finds that about a third of those interviewed do not speak to their fathers at all, with only around 10 per cent of men seeing themselves as having a deep and long-lasting relationship with their dads.

It's clear to me that fathers do well when they work hard to establish and grow their relationships with their children. As we all know, we are not flawless, and mistakes are made. But, for the most part, if children know they are loved and have a secure life, those are the roots from which they can build their lives. We can think of times with our fathers or male role models who have spent time with us, helped us and guided our ways. I am grateful to my dad for the way he patiently tried to help me with my maths homework. As someone not naturally gifted in that side of things, I did appreciate it, especially as he had a demanding work life alongside regular commitments volunteering for the local community. As parents to two children, Tony and I, whilst not perfect, have always tried to build a good and affirming relationship with them. As they have grown up, we are now enjoying the benefits of that bond.

'The Pursuit of Happyness' is an American movie released in 2006. It tells the story of a struggling salesman who becomes homeless with his young son, Christopher. Despite facing numerous challenges, Chris never gives up on his dream of providing a better life for his son. Ultimately, he achieves his dream of becoming a successful stockbroker with his son by his side. This is based on a true story, and the real Chris Gardner features very briefly near the film's ending.

Sadly, others have different stories about growing up with their fathers. I invite you to hear the stories of some well-known names to help you understand why this is the case.

The British actor Alan Cumming had a very insecure and troubled start in life which has shaped him and impacted him. Both he and his brother had a very tough childhood. Their father was violent emotionally and physically towards them: "There is not one memory from our childhoods that is not clouded by fear or humiliation or pain", he wrote in his memoir, 'Not My Father's Son'. In an interview on BBC Radio 4's Desert Island Discs in March 2022, Cummings talked openly about his painful upbringing and revealed: "My dad told me I was worthless, my mum told me I was precious."[6]

In Sir Elton John's autobiography, 'Me', he writes honestly about his difficult upbringing with both his parents. His Dad "...was a typical British man of the fifties in that he seemed to regard any display of emotion, other than anger, as evidence of a fatal weakness of character ... he never told you he loved you ... but ... if he heard me playing the piano, I'd get a 'well done', maybe an arm around the shoulder, a sense of pride and approval." Elton John describes that being in his father's (and mother's) good books was significant to him.[7]

It is interesting to get different views on what it is to be noticed. Brian May, lead guitarist and songwriter from the globally renowned and hugely successful rock band Queen, has been open about his relationship with his father.[8] He had previously been a teacher and an expert in physics. His father had never understood his decision to give all that up and join a band. May's father didn't go to a concert until Queen played at the impressive Maddison Gardens venue in New York. Afterwards, his dad told him, "I get it." Brian May was visibly moved as he recalled the story, saying it was as if he had been waiting for that "seal of approval".

A Balancing Act

Being noticed and affirmed is not the same as always being praised, which is sometimes a criticism aimed at parents or caregivers of children in today's world. Certainly, spoiling children or not giving them boundaries and discipline can have dangers, too. We all need to be wary of it. However, it is not just an issue in modern society.

That Famous Coat

I am reminded of the biblical character Joseph in the Old Testament. Many have heard of him because of the West End show 'Joseph and the Amazing Technicolor Dreamcoat' and the memorable songs that resulted from it. The story comes from Genesis 37.

"Now Israel (Jacob) loved Joseph more than any of his other sons, because he had been born to him in his old age, and he made an ornate robe for him. When his brothers saw that their father loved him more than any of them, they hated him and could not speak a kind word to him."

Due to their jealousy, Joseph's brothers sold him into slavery and then pretended to their father that he had been killed. Joseph was very special to his ageing father. It appears he was arrogant and boastful, and he had to learn some hard lessons that shaped his character for good. Eventually, he became a great leader.

In March 2024, Kevin Maher, the Times and Sunday Times columnist, author and film critic, wrote about the contrasts in approach to parenting and used the example of David Beckham and his father, Ted. Beckham said his father taught him the value of hard work, discipline and humility. But he rarely got a "well done" from him.   Maher writes, "It was only after earning his hundredth cap for England that Ted finally broke with years of stern parenting protocol to deliver actual praise, saying, 'You've made it, boy.'" He continues: "It must be mightily perplexing for a child today, slowly emerging into self-awareness and thinking, 'Wait a minute. I am the best at every sport I've ever tried? I am the most accomplished musician ... the most gifted artist ... and the most academically adept child on the planet. Something's not quite right here. I don't feel good.'"[9]

Maher concludes, "And what replaces praise? You pick up your child, pull them in close and tell them that you love them deeply, that you're forever changed because of them, but that they really need to work on their draftsmanship. Something like that. Ask Ted Beckham. He knows."

Alan, Elton, Brian and David. All are incredibly successful, hugely talented and admired worldwide. Still, they are also ordinary humans who handle family pressures and issues. It is good to learn about the real person behind the success and glamour of fame. It reminds us that we are all shaped by our early childhood experiences and memories. Furthermore, I can see both sides of the story and agree with Kevin Maher's views about those who heap praise upon praise on their children are not doing them any favours for their future. A balanced approach is the most ideal — "boundaries with kindness" is a phrase I've heard used and rather like.

When children are little, they look up to their parents, regardless of whether the parent feels like they are doing well in their role. P. Fontaine tells the story of a little boy who was unusually alone with his dad at bedtime.[10] After having a lot of fun playing together, the father was about to lift him into bed when the son declared it was time to say his prayers. The child recited his usual evening prayer; then he added something else: "Dear God, make me a big, good man, like my daddy. Amen." Very soon after that, he was asleep. His father knelt by his son's bedside and prayed, "Dear Lord, make me a great, big, good man like my boy thinks I am."

Overcoming the Odds

The former professional footballer and TV pundit Ian Wright has spoken candidly about his difficult start in life.[11] Wright's father left when he was very young; he only saw him fleetingly throughout his childhood. Wright describes waiting for his dad, who promised to bring him some money for some needed clothes. He was due to turn up in the morning, so he waited and waited. Eventually, later that afternoon, his father arrived. Wright's emotions were in turmoil, but he had already promised himself that he would never have anything to do with him again if his father hadn't turned up.

Into this difficult situation stepped Mr Pigden, a schoolteacher, who noticed this young, troubled pupil at school, enabling Wright to set out on a different path and direction with hard work and perseverance. Ian Wright was emotional, recalling how this teacher had given him tasks to do in school, trusting him with more and more responsibility, and invested in him, encouraging him to pursue his love of football. Years later, after Wright had retired from professional football with a distinguished and successful career behind him, he unexpectedly met Mr Pigden again. The old man hugged him and told him how proud he was of him. "I know he loved me," Wright says. "He was the first imposing male figure in my life trying to guide me on the right road."

This story is about overcoming the odds and achieving something despite a challenging childhood. This boy needed to be noticed, loved and affirmed. It turned his life around for the better, and someone other than his father provided that.

That resonates with many people who must find a way to get through; finding within themselves tools to cope: resilience, grit, character and hope. David Sedaris is an American comedian, author and radio contributor who experienced a difficult childhood with his father: "As long as my father had power, he used it to hurt me." Sedaris said his father would constantly say to him, "You are a big fat zero."[12] Although his father did soften towards the end of his life, Sedaris has used many of his harrowing experiences in his writing and live comedy shows, as he knows many people have had a difficult parent growing up and could probably relate to some of his experiences.

Sometimes, we can't understand how we have been treated, but it can impact us as adults. How much better would it be to have someone to guide you, mentor and encourage you, and give you an order and framework within which to grow and flourish?

I expect you are familiar with the term "County Lines", which is essentially a term describing how criminal gangs exploit vulnerable children and young people and manipulate them into becoming drug dealers, often inflicting violence and trauma onto these young lives. These groups not only make it appear to be worth their while but also give them a sense of belonging, purpose, and affirmation — however shallow and misconstrued.

I heard Phoebe McIndoe, the award-winning radio producer, describe her first-hand experience with the issues, as her brother had become involved with County Lines.[13] She knew how tough it can be to escape a life of debt bondage. When her brother tried to leave the gang, their house was burgled, so he returned to the fold. "Although my parents started paying for his freedom, the debt bond wouldn't break," she said.

McIndoe spoke to those caught up in these gangs and investigated why it's incredibly hard to break the cycle. One young man grew up in a home where his mother had left when he was very young, and he was physically and mentally abused by his stepmother. All these things made him a vulnerable target to the older children around him, who could manipulate him, teaching him how to use a firearm and how to deal drugs at a young age.

There are those who are trying to help change the prospects of the most vulnerable. Still, with cutbacks in funding youth groups and outreach workers, gangs are a strong force on social media and are hard to resist. I was encouraged to learn about the work of the Violence Reduction Unit (VRU) in London and how they support initiatives that mainly work with estranged dads trying to re-build relationships with their children, whether their absence is due to serving a prison sentence or who are separated from the mother of their children.

A Thought for Today
Fathers, Sons and Father Figures

Acknowledgement should go to those who work to support men in becoming better dads, especially to help those who grew up without a dad themselves. I also applaud the good, trustworthy and faithful father figures in boys' lives — the teachers, cub and scout leaders, charity workers, Sunday school teachers, football coaches, godparents, and tutors — who positively impact their future direction.

In the New Testament, Paul is regarded as an inspirational trailblazer to many, especially as he and his companions had planted churches. These were where new Christian leaders learnt how to build and maintain a faith community. In the letter to the church in Thessalonica, Paul, Silas and Timothy give thanks for the people growing in faith through instruction, prayer and example: "For you know that we dealt with each of you as a father deals with his own children, encouraging, comforting and urging you to live lives worthy of God, who calls you into His kingdom and glory" (1 Thessalonians 2:11–12).

- Consider someone who has influenced you in your life. Take a moment to express your gratitude in your heart (or, if appropriate, with a message or a phone call).

- This is an opportune time to reflect on how, where, and to whom we might serve as positive role models and mentors.

FRANCES MILES

Chapter 8
Mothers, Fathers, Sons and Daughters

It has been said that children get their nurturing from their mother and their identity from their father. Yes, not all mothers and fathers have stereotypical qualities. Still, children usually begin their lives with a physical and emotional connection to their mothers, which is hopefully strengthened and nourished over the years.

I have already mentioned John Wesley, the Anglican Priest who founded the Methodist movement. Here is his backstory: He was born to Samuel and Susanna in 1703. When he was five, local villagers miraculously saved him from the family home when it caught fire. His mother's Christian teaching profoundly influenced Wesley (more than his father, Samuel, a clergyman). John, the son Susanna described as "the brand, plucked from the burning", once wrote: "I learned more about Christianity from my mother than from all the theologians of England."

It was a large family. Samuel and Susanna had 19 children, but only ten survived to adulthood. Despite her husband's frequent absences, Susanna set aside specific times in the week to talk and pray with each child. She also would read Bible passages with them every morning and evening. Although today's standards could consider her a rather harsh disciplinarian, Mary Greetham, in her book 'Susanna Wesley, Mother of Methodism', writes that Susanna should be judged against her times and consider that her influence on her children was lasting. "She constantly prayed (for her children) and kept up a lively correspondence with them throughout her life."

Never underestimate the power of a woman of prayer! I am thankful to have a mum who has prayed for me and my siblings and continues to do so, along with the wider extended family that keeps growing. I also count my blessings that my in-laws were wonderfully supportive. I was just 18 when I got engaged to my husband. We were attending a Methodist Bible College in Derbyshire at the time. Soon after our engagement was announced, I received a letter in the post that began: "When my boys were small, I often wondered what their wives would be like and how awful it would be if I did not like their choice. I need not have worried. From the day you came into Anthony's life, I liked you and have grown to love you."

That letter meant so much to me, more than my mother-in-law would have realised. I knew I was wonderfully accepted into the Miles family. Regrettably, Pat died of cancer in her 50s. Still, I kept the letter in her lovely, neat handwriting and will always treasure it.

One of Those Days

I have become more aware of my shortcomings and failings as I've grown older. If you have a family around you, it is not easy to cover up those foibles or pretend you are totally coping with life when that isn't the whole picture. However, receiving expressions of love from children is delightful and comforting to know that perhaps you're not doing too badly. One Mothering Sunday, along with the cards, I was given a voucher for a pamper session. I was very much looking forward to it.

The day arrived; it was a Saturday morning and time was tight. I had to visit the post office first and then head to the salon at the other end of High Street. As I made my way to the appointment, I rummaged for the voucher in my bag to ensure I had it ready to hand in. Despite a thorough search, the voucher was nowhere to be found, so I turned around and retraced my steps back to the post office. Frustratingly, I still couldn't find the vital piece of paper. As time passed, I started to get anxious as I dislike being late.

I turned up late for the appointment — without the voucher, apologising profusely. At this point, I was more than a little hot and bothered! Thankfully, it wasn't a problem, and I was led into a cosy, softly lit room. The calming "sounds of the sea" music was playing in the background, and the soft lighting with a fragrant flickering candle enabled me to take a deep breath and try to relax. I lay face down on the bed, ready for a nice shoulder massage. Fantastic, I have made it at last. Now for some "me time".

Then my phone rang. It was too far away to reach easily, but I did my best to try and retrieve it. With my arm stretched as far as possible, the ringing stopped just as I was about to grab the phone. Doing my best to get back into a relaxed position, all was fine until... the ringing began again. This time, I was worried, so I got up and managed to pick up the call. It was my husband, wondering where I was. He had forgotten I had gone out for my relaxing treat.

The therapist began to massage my shoulders as I returned to where I should have been. "Hmm," she said. "You're a bit tense."

Fathers and Daughters

The twenty-three-year-old Paralympian swimmer, Louise Fiddes, was about to be interviewed by a sports correspondent after winning a gold medal at the Paris Paralympic Games in 2024. He noticed her intently looking up at the noisy supporters cheering her achievement. "You were looking for your dad in the crowd," he observed. Louise replied: "He's always been here for me, even from a little kid. There's not been a single day that he hasn't believed I can get gold. I can't wait to see him!"

Eleanor Anstruther, a best-selling British novelist, once shared a heartbreaking but equally beautiful story, "As a child, I made a Valentine's card for my dad. I was proud of it, but he discarded it without care. I was devastated. It set me off on a lifetime of proving I was good enough. Then, my brother sent a file of things our dad had kept. In it was the card. He had kept the card."[14]

Louise and Eleanor are two daughters with loving fathers. The trouble is that Eleanor didn't hear what she needed as a girl, which impacted her self-esteem and confidence. Conversely, I wonder if Paralympian medallist Louise would have won her breaststroke race in Paris without her father's continuing encouragement and belief in her.

It has been a longstanding tradition at British weddings for fathers to accompany their daughters on the journey to the ceremony and to walk down the aisle with her before "giving her away". Those customs might be changing these days, but it is still quite common for dads to speak about their daughters in a speech. This invariably includes funny stories and memories, but there is also an opportunity for a father to tell his daughter how proud he is of her as a person and how special she is to him. It isn't currently the norm (within the usual traditions of a British wedding) for a dad to do the same for a son on his wedding day. Perhaps there should be — that could potentially be very empowering!

I am so grateful that my husband and I have had the privilege of being parents, something that I never take for granted, mindful of many who, for whatever reason, have been unable to have children. Navigating the joys, the challenges, the overwhelming emotions and the broken nights as a parent or stepparent isn't always easy. And now, as a grandparent, when the responsibility for the children is much less, but the love is still so strong, I sometimes reflect that I could have handled things more patiently or spent more quality time with my two when they were younger. My parents-in-law had a fridge magnet, which always made me smile: "If I had known grandkids were so much fun, I would have had them first." However, I have always believed that the most important thing was that our children knew we loved them. As a couple, we endeavoured to support our children's activities and interests as best we could, creating memories along the way.

Making Memories

In March 2000, Tony took our then-eight-year-old daughter to her first concert at Earls Court, London. It was to see her favourite pop band, the Spice Girls. Of course, thousands of enthusiastic children were there too, dressed up to identify with their favourite Spice Girl.

Near the end of the concert, Tony told a disappointed Hannah they needed to go and to follow him. They pushed and snaked their way through the heaving crowd, and Hannah was gutted that they were leaving early. Her daddy said, "Just trust me" and he managed to get to the side of the stage just as the pop stars were heading off backstage. Hannah started waving enthusiastically, and they all noticed her and waved back. Wow, what a thrill for our girl. Now, as a mum of three, she looks back on that special time with her dad and is successfully passing on her passion for music to the next generation.

Sometimes, it can be very challenging to raise a family. I came across the story of a humble Methodist itinerant minister from the 1800s who was often discouraged. "The work was hard; the compensation meagre. How many times he was tempted to give up! Three daughters grew up to young womanhood in that home. Over time, all three were married. One became the mother of a celebrated artist; one was the mother of Stanley Baldwin, Prime Minister; the other was the mother of Rudyard Kipling, the famous novelist."

A Thought for Today
Making the Most of the Testing Times

Looking back can be challenging when we reflect on our time as parents, godparents, or caregivers and think about how we should have done things differently, given more attention, or set more explicit boundaries for the children in our lives. Feeling guilty can be overwhelming, but so can our opportunities to change the here, now, and future when we resolve to do things better.

- Maybe this is an opportunity to think about the present and how we interact with those closest to us.

- Are we intentionally carving out quality time with the generations above, around and below us? We won't have them with us forever! Read Ecclesiastes 3: "There is a time for everything..."

ROOTED, LOVED, AFFIRMED

FRANCES MILES

Chapter 9
A Wider and Longer Perspective

Peering Through the Pier

When our children were around four and two, I took them with a friend and her little boy to Clacton — a traditional seaside town in Essex. In the afternoon, we decided to walk along the wooden pier to get a view of the sea and coastline. The children, however, spent most of their time sprawled on their tummies, looking through the tiny gaps between the planks of wood. They were intrigued by the glimpses of the dark, cold, swirling water beneath them. They were much more interested in that than gazing at the vast expanse of glistening (well, at least I think it was glistening!) sea all around them.

Observing the three young kids lying flat out, squinting through the cracks, was endearing and slightly comical. I'm glad they found it so fascinating. Still, I felt they were also missing out on taking in the sheer vastness of the ocean and all the variety of colour and power on display as the waves crashed onto the beach. There is a broader picture. Our vast, beautiful world is in trouble, and we shouldn't be tempted to narrow our vision and focus solely on the small circle around us and our families while ignoring the broader and wider issues.

Looking Back: The Second World War

When war was declared in September 1939, 1.5 million evacuees were sent from towns and cities in the UK to safer parts of the country. Further evacuations followed a few years later when Germany attacked areas in the east and southeast of England. It must have been a frightening and confusing time for the children who were sent away from their families, as well as for those who were left behind. There would have been a constant fear of attack and an ongoing concern for loved ones living far away. The unfortunate fact is we only have to watch or read news bulletins today to witness the impact of war on people coping with separation, fear and the loss of security as they are forced to leave their homes and flee to a place of safety.

The famous British "keep calm and carry on" spirit was a huge motivator in the war years to encourage people to get on and work together to help the war effort. Some research suggests that perhaps suppressing feelings and emotions for the greater good may have impacted people's well-being in the following years. The English actor and comedian Adrian Edmondson shared an example of this. He was appearing on an episode of BBC Radio 4's Desert Island Discs and recalled what happened on his seventh birthday. He went to kiss his father "goodnight", but his father replied: "Now you're seven, I think we can forget all this kissing thing and we'll just shake hands."[14]

Edmondson recalled that it seemed a very reasonable idea at the time. Still, he has replayed that incident many times since then, and it has had a lasting impact on him. Edmondson did concede that his father had been brought up in the shadow of World War Two and the Blitz, which could partly explain why his dad couldn't connect emotionally with his son.

In the UK, we have a reminder at the annual Remembrance services and festivals in early November to take in and consider not only the considerable loss of young servicemen in both world wars but the impact it would have had on the immediate families and society. An elderly World War Two Veteran was interviewed about his recollections of the D-Day landings on the beaches of Normandy in June 1944. He had a different role that day but was near enough to the action to witness those who bravely disembarked from boats and clambered onto the sand at enormous risk to their own lives. Many men were killed that day. "I'm 100, and I've had a life," he said, "Not like those who died on the beaches. They didn't have a life, only their youth."

The trauma and impact of the loss of a generation of young men in British society was massive. Still, it was more than just loss that caused an upheaval: The Royal British Legion states that "new families were created as women married servicemen of other nations and moved overseas; children were born in fatherless homes as a result of demobilised troops leaving the UK to return to the US or Canada or due to a death as a result of the war; and the divorce rate spiked as many families struggled to re-adjust to a world at peace."

Like many from the Baby Boomer generation and beyond, I have parents born in the late 1930s–40s. It's worth considering the impact of hardship, rationing, loss and separation on that generation growing up. This might explain why some people are uncomfortable displaying love or affection. Some believe it has swung the other way, with today's generation of young parents perhaps being too indulgent and demonstrative in showing love to their children.

The Windrush Generations and the Barrel Children

Of course, it wasn't just the evacuations in World War Two that impacted families. Some were called the Windrush Generation — people who migrated to the UK from Caribbean Commonwealth countries between 1948 and 1973 to fill post-war labour shortages and rebuild the economy.

Nadine White wrote a piece for The Independent.[15] She interviewed Jennifer Pringle, who experienced the loss of her mother as a toddler when she travelled from Jamaica to Britain. After being brought up by her grandmother, Pringle travelled to the UK, aged 14, to rejoin her mother, who lived in the West Midlands. The emotional toll on Pringle was long-lasting. "I love my Mother, but I never truly felt wanted," she says. "And I am still working through the trauma."

White writes: "It is estimated that during the peak period of the migration, between 1955 and 1960, adults brought 6,500 children with them but left 90,000 behind in the Caribbean. The term 'barrel children' was coined by Jamaican academic Dr Claudette Crawford-Brown in the 1990s, and is defined as those who, while waiting in the Caribbean to follow their parents to America and the UK, received food and clothing 'in lieu of direct care.'"

The article highlights that feelings of low self-esteem and sadness have had a lasting impact on some of the children involved. There are deep, significant issues as governments, authorities, or parents decide what seems right for the family in difficult circumstances. There are terrible and terrifying situations across the world where families are faced with difficult choices. We celebrate the great work of women and men over the years and generations who have stood up to help and highlight the issues that affect children.

A Global Perspective: Serving with Love in São Paulo

Brazil's largest city, São Paulo, as in many places in the world, has extremes of wealth and poverty. Children born into hardship are much more likely to encounter violence and crime growing up and often become involved themselves. My fantastic friend, Cally Magalhães, left her home in Milton Keynes and began her ministry there in 1999, initially working with street children. She now runs an organisation called The Eagle Project. It supports youth prisoners (mainly teenage boys) to leave a life of crime and get an education or find work instead. Cally and her team use a method called psychodrama, where the boys take on the role of their victims, the victim's family members or their relatives. These workshops held in prisons are having a significant impact on young people and the future choices they make.

In her book 'Dancing With Thieves', Cally introduces us to Alexandre: "We lived in a really poor neighbourhood, and life was very hard," he says. His mother was just 14 when she fell pregnant with him, and he doesn't know who his father is. "Right from when I was young, everybody hit me: my mum, my grandmother, my aunties and my cousins... As I was beaten so much, I behaved the same way and started hitting the children at school. I realise now I would just lash out in anger for what I was going through at home."[16]

Alexandre soon got into more trouble in and out of school, and by the age of eleven, he had stolen his first motorbike. Soon, he was stealing many motorbikes a day and robbing people at gunpoint. He and a friend then progressed to robbing supermarkets and cars. Initially reluctant to take part in the drama sessions in youth prison, this young man came to realise the impact of his actions.

Through help, support and love from Cally and her team, Alexandre came out of prison and began working as a hairdresser. Starting off cutting hair in his grandmother's garage, this young man is now a very successful barber with his own salon and gives courses on how to be a barber. His dream is to help poor boys in his neighbourhood and steer them away from a life of crime.

Rights of the Child

In 1924, Eglatyne Jebb, the founder of Save the Children, drafted the first Declaration of the Rights of the Child. Today, children's rights are still grossly violated worldwide.

She stated:

1. Every child should be given what they need to grow up happy and healthy.

2. When a child is hungry, they must be fed. When they are sick, they must be cared for. And when they need support, shelter or guidance, they must be given it.

3. Whenever there is a crisis, children should be the first to receive aid.

4. Every child should be protected against exploitation, and given the chance to earn a living, when the time comes.

5. Every child should grow up understanding the importance of using their talents and skills to help others.

What was true in 1924 is still relevant to us over 100 years later. One in six of the world's children live in a conflict zone, according to official data from 2022–2024. Through my reading and reflection, I am learning that contrary to the view that children are the future (with apologies to the writers of the wonderful song 'Greatest Love of All'), they are also our present. We should weep as we see how little innocent ones are exploited, traumatised and mistreated, caught up in situations that are not their own doing. We should do all we can to protect, nurture and guide children, giving them a safe structure and framework to grow, learn and flourish.

We Write Off Vulnerable Children at Our Peril

The musical production 'Les Misérables' is truly remarkable. It is based on Victor Hugo's book, published in 1862. The backdrop to the book is the French Revolution and the years that followed — one of the most turbulent and violent periods in the country's history. In his preface to the book, Hugo declares that stories like his needed to be written whilst the three problems of the age existed: "the degradation of man by poverty, the ruin of woman by starvation and the dwarfing of childhood by physical and spiritual night".

In the novel, Gavroche is introduced as a boy living on Paris' streets. He has very little, but despite this, he lives by his wits and shows kindness to those he encounters: "...he had a father and a mother. But his father did not think of him, and his mother did not love him. He was one of those children most deserving of pity among all, one of those who have a father and mother, and who are orphans nonetheless."

In his book, 'Will You Join in Our Crusade', Steve Mann used the inspiration of Les Misérables to uncover the truths in the gospels.[17] He says of Garoche, "If he were alive today, he would no doubt be viewed by society as an anti-social nuisance, yet he is also the proverbial street urchin with a heart of gold ... he has a strong sense of justice. He helps out an old man with no money ... he even helps his enemies when help is needed."

Mann then compares the situation when children were being brought to Jesus to be blessed, but his disciples tried to keep them at bay. Jesus instead asked the children to come to Him, "for the kingdom of God belongs to such as these."

Mann says: "Children, like Gavroche, are nowhere near perfect, but it is their intuitive qualities to which Jesus is alluding. These can disappear with the clutter of adulthood." This challenges me to consider how, as an adult in my spheres of influence, I can help protect the innocent, enable children to be children and help them grow in their understanding of God's love for them and what the Kingdom of God can offer them.

Influencers

Just as in the story of a flour-covered miller who left his mark on everyone he touched as he edged his way through a crowded place, as a Christian, I am called to have an impact in today's world. The presence of influencers on social media is a modern phenomenon. Christians are also in that space and able to share testimonies and words of Scripture alongside those who are perhaps just out for material gain and "superstar" status.

Despite the lure of all that smartphones have to offer, children are still influenced by their parents by observing what they say and what they do. My daughter told me when she was a teenager that she didn't feel tempted to swear because we didn't. That doesn't mean a young person's peer group isn't very influential either. Still, I think parents forget how much children observe how we treat one another in the home, how we react to things, especially when life isn't going so well, and how we handle conflict and disputes.

Thought for Today
The Challenge to be A Good Influencer and A Good Neighbour

My father-in-law, Jim, was a respected and successful business and training consultant. He was a fan of Dale Carnegie, who wrote the best-selling book, 'How to Win Friends and Influence People'. This book, published in 1936, has sold over 30 million copies. Carnegie wrote: "The world is full of people who are grabbing and self-seeking. So the rare individual who unselfishly tries to serve others has an enormous advantage."

- Would I be happy to be considered an influencer or worry if others imitated my words and actions? Would I measure up to my own high standards and the even higher standards of the Christian faith?

- Each child, indeed, each human life, is precious. Who are the lost people we walk past or quickly forget? How wide and deep is our love for the world? Jesus' parable of the Good Samaritan in Luke 10 challenged His hearers to think beyond the obvious boundaries. Perhaps today, it will prompt the discerning reader to consider who their neighbour is.

We will likely interact with others day-to-day, whether briefly in a shop or more intently in a conversation with a friend or loved one. Let us explore the power and influence of spoken and written words in our daily lives.

Chapter 10
Words, Words, Words

"Words kill, words give life; they're either poison or fruit you choose"
(Proverbs 18:21).

Words directed towards us can build us up or bring us down. I mentioned earlier a man who appeared on a reality TV series. He had been reluctant to share the layers of hurts he had built up over many years. But he did reveal that he was there just before his father had died. "I don't like you" were his father's final words and parting gift to his son — if you could ever call it that.

The trouble is that messages like that can strike like a dagger to the heart. For the most part, we have a choice about what to say and how to express it. Typically, an adult in the UK knows between 20,000 and 35,000 words, so we have plenty to choose from. Speech is one form, but of course, there are words we can craft into a text message, an inspiring poem, a song, or a memorable letter.

Words On A Page

Our daughter was embarking on the most significant journey of her life. She was heading to the USA to make the final preparations to marry her American fiancé, whom she had met a few years earlier while he was on a college placement in the UK.

It had been a full-on and challenging 12 months for this young couple, separated by thousands of miles and the Atlantic Ocean in between. Still, as we stood by the check-in area with Hannah at Heathrow, we knew the threads were coming together, and they would soon marry. We would meet again for the wedding ceremony in just over a week. As we said our long and rather emotional goodbyes, Hannah handed us an envelope with the words on the front: "To Mum and Dad... to open on my departure. Yes, this may well be a huge bill, which I accumulated over 21 years." Despite the ominous warning, inside was a card in which our wonderful daughter had written a list of thanks to us for several things over her life. "This is just a little keepsake letter of my appreciation," it began. And that is what it has been — a comfort and a joy to return to now and then. Over 12 years later, and through all the ups and downs of life, I am pleased that our daughter is making a life for herself, albeit in another country. She and her wonderful husband, Dominic, now have three children. We miss them all, but I am thankful to have Hannah's handwritten words to read, and to make me smile.

Having an attitude of gratitude to the generations above us, around us or below us is no bad thing!

Tony Castle shares this anonymous tale: "A young man heard with disgust that his wealthy old uncle had left him a Bible in his will. The will read thus: 'To my nephew, I leave a copy of God's priceless word, which I trust he will use daily and find within its pages real treasure.' The beneficiary threw the Bible into an old trunk in the attic, disgusted and disappointed with his share in his uncle's bequests. Years later, at a time of depression, he turned to the good Book for comfort. Between its pages, he found many thousands of pounds."

Be Careful!

In Proverbs 25:11, there is this delightful thought: "The right word at the right time is like precious gold set in silver." I read that children and young people hear approximately 18 negative statements for every one life-giving comment. How can we, as adults, impact our children and young people? It is not only what people hear but also how and when they say things.

I heard about a football match played by eight and nine-year-old boys. Through a large part of the game, one of the fathers, standing on the sidelines, barked instructions at his child and told him in no uncertain terms when and how he was getting it wrong. At one point, the dad got so exasperated with his son's performance that he shouted, "Why aren't you listening to me?!" The young footballer stopped and told his father he was trying to listen and do his best. He was finding it hard to play the game with all the commands. At the end of the match, the youngsters went over to those watching, as they usually did, to receive the praise and "well done" — whatever the result was that day. The father didn't applaud his boy.

Be Intentional

A preacher was talking about the power of words and how the meaning and timing of spoken words were impactful. He was urging the congregation to be impulsive with life-enhancing words and encouragement. He then presented a challenge: "How many boys and men would just love to hear their dad say, 'I'm proud of you?'"

I am sure that would be a large number. God the Father knew what He was doing to express His satisfaction with Jesus at that time and place in His life. How much more do we, as weak and sinful human beings, need to be reminded of this as parents and, indeed, children?

Specific Praise

But this is not just about close family relationships. When training to be a manager, I remember being taught that it was essential to "catch people in the act of doing something great" and mention it there and then or at least refer to it at an appropriate time soon afterwards.

Praising someone for a specific reason is a good practice to cultivate... "Sue, I overheard you on the phone this morning and felt you handled that complaint well. You listened, you calmly repeated back what the issue was with the customer, you offered an apology, and then you suggested how the situation could be resolved. Excellent work!" This is much more impactful than: "Well done, Sue, you're doing a great job." Although not wrong, the latter comment could soon be received like water off a duck's back if repeated too frequently.

"Kind Words Are the Music of the World"

Frederick William Faber (1814–1863) was an English hymn writer and theologian. He wrote: "Kind words are the music of the world. They have a power which seems to be beyond natural causes, as if they were some angel's song, which had lost its way and come on earth, and sang on undyingly, smiting the hearts of men with sweetest wounds, and putting for a while an angel's nature into us."

Showing kindness through our words is one way to demonstrate to the people in our lives that we see them, notice them, and appreciate them. In other words, we affirm them!

The Answer to My Question

You may recall that near the beginning of the book, I recounted the occasion when I visited my parents for a specific purpose. I finally plucked up the courage to ask them a seemingly trivial question that lingered in my mind for a long time.

"Were You Disappointed When I Was Born?"

As the third of three daughters, followed later by our brother, I looked for even a flicker between them as if they might have been waiting to hear my question. But no exchange of glances, just an immediate and sincere response, with some surprise that I had even raised this. Their reply was earnest: "Not at all! We accepted whatever we were given. There was not a thought about disappointment. We love you very much."

Thank you, Mum and Dad. I've never doubted your love for me. I just needed to hear your answer.

"Wise words are like deep waters — bringing refreshment, cleansing, cooling and life" (Proverbs 18:4).

I am a daughter, a wife, a mother, a grandmother, a sister, a sister-in-law, a niece, an auntie, a great auntie, a friend and a godmother. I feel a responsibility within those roles to be careful with what I say and how I say it and to handle relationships respectfully, even in the heat of the moment. As someone who occasionally speaks before thinking (I prefer the phrase that I tend to "speak with my heart"), that isn't necessarily easy!

A Thought for Today
Words Used for Good

- How do I express my faith and love language to those in my family and extended circle to enable them to grow, flourish and mature?
- Am I sowing seeds of love and encouragement to enable roots to develop and grow stronger?
- Am I really listening to what someone is saying to me?
- Am I using words to nurture, acknowledge, challenge, and sometimes correct, but always to point to a greater love — a more profound and wonderful love that brings hope to the world?

This verse from a hymn is perhaps something to ponder as I go about my daily activities and interactions with the people I encounter:

"May the Mind of Christ my Saviour,
Live in me from day to day,
By His love and power controlling
All I do or say."
Katie Barclay Wilkinson (1859–1928)

FRANCES MILES

Chapter 11
Let's Get Practical

As I've been writing, I've considered what we can do in our everyday lives to show others love, kindness and humanity. We recognise that as human beings, we need to know who we are and be loved and acknowledged.

In the book 'The Money Devotional', Mark Lloydbottom writes: "Children soak up parental attitudes and behavioural traits like a sponge soaks up water. Children have more need of good role models than of critics."

Here are a few practical ways we might adopt to become good role models to those in our circle of family and friendships:

Demonstrating Love

Demonstrating you love someone can be hard to do. I've observed that in some families when they get together, the female members are greeted with a kiss or a hug. In contrast, adult men will limit the contact to a shake of the hands or a grip on the arm. How about we change that and be more comfortable with hugs? I think that for this one, gentlemen, it's over to you! I know it isn't easy, and indeed, there are times when it isn't appropriate, but it is worth considering. I remember my father-in-law, who had been widowed in his 50s, would say that he appreciated a hug when we went to visit him. It meant a lot and comforted him, especially in his last years when he was frail with Parkinson's.

Someone once said, "Hugs are not just for saying hello or goodbye. They're the silent way of saying you matter to me."

Resolving To Do Things Better

A 22-year-old expectant father had grown up without ever meeting his father, so he decided that he would not repeat the past. Instead, he wanted to be as present as possible for his child, no matter how challenging that might be. That young man was determined that his child wouldn't grow up with resentment in his heart as he did. Of course, we don't know why things may have happened to us in the past, but this illustrates a mature approach to learning lessons and resolving not to repeat past mistakes but to strive to do better. Does this prompt you to consider how a change in one or two areas of your life might significantly impact others and their futures?

Say Their Name

I know it is obvious, but even if we have a popular first name, it belongs to us, and it was the first gift we were given! Names are unique to you and me. I am not always that great at remembering someone's name. One thing I try to do, though, is to remember something about the person. This can prompt me to recall the name when I next see them. Or even better, if I try to listen well enough in the first place, I should be able to note it and remember it!

Whilst he was in hospital for a few days, my husband made sure he read the name badges of the various staff members who came in. He wrote them down. When they returned the next time, he would intentionally use their names to thank them, whether it was the orderly, the surgeon, the physio, or the nurse.

Calling someone by their name can be powerfully enhancing. It may be the first time they have heard it said out loud that day or week.

Pausing Before Speaking

As a Rotarian, I like the "Rotary Four-Way Test" which is a set of questions that can be used as a moral compass to guide decisions in both personal and professional life:

- Is it the truth?
- Is it fair to all concerned?
- Will it build goodwill and better friendships?
- Will it be beneficial to all concerned?

It is often recited at the start of meetings, as it can help people stop and think before giving their opinions. It can be beneficial to apply this to different areas of our lives, pausing to consider the words we speak or actions we decide to take... or not take.

Dealing With Phones — Put Them Away and GFA!

This is hard for many of those who are on their phones a lot. I get it. I am, too — I use it for all sorts of things, but it can, as most of us will be aware, become an addiction. When sharing a meal or speaking to a loved one, why not try putting the phone away and giving that person your full attention? Even if we can do two things simultaneously, it can be off-putting if someone thinks you're not interested in what they are saying because you are scrolling through a phone.

On a related point, I've had the experience of talking to someone when they were looking past me — I suspect they were more interested in speaking to another person instead! It's not the most encouraging thing to experience. I try to practice the art of GFA: giving full attention.

We Don't Have To Be Picture Perfect

It makes me mad and indeed sad that today, younger generations are bombarded with messages on how to have the perfect pout, a flawless body, the ideal weight, the most blemish-free skin, and a Hollywood-worthy smile. I am disappointed that even in these "enlightened times", I see photos of some female "A-listers" appearing in public with the skimpiest of outfits.

I sound like a real prude, but I'm not. I'm just a grandmother to four little girls, concerned about the world they are growing up in. The message society often gives young women is that what they are born with is not good enough or sufficiently beautiful to be acceptable, so it needs to be enhanced.

We all know how difficult and dangerous it can be to navigate the world of social media, especially with the issues surrounding sexting and bullying. Instead, I wish there was as much attention given to how people can enhance beauty on the inside. The Bible tells us that the fruits of the Spirit are love, joy, peace, patience, kindness, goodness, faithfulness, gentleness, and self-control (Galatians 5:22). We can't attain these in our own strength. We need God to work in our lives through the Holy Spirit to help cultivate and grow these qualities.

If you have daughters, granddaughters, or other young people in your life and feel as passionately about them as I do, then let's work together to try and turn the tide on "picture-perfect-ness". We could show that there is a better and more fulfilled way to live — even with a physical imperfection here and there.

Many years ago, God tasked the Old Testament prophet Samuel to anoint a new king of Israel. He was sent to Bethlehem, to the home of Jesse, who had eight sons. Each son came to meet Samuel, but none of them were chosen: "The Lord does not look at the things people look at. People look at the outward appearance, but the Lord looks at the heart" (1 Samuel 16:7). In the end it was the youngest boy, David, working outside looking after the sheep, who was God's chosen one to be king. That Bible verse still seems so relevant these days.

Learning To Let Go and Let God...

...is hard to do, especially when your 17-year-old daughter has her driving test in the morning. Then, that afternoon, she drives her brother to football training. It was a "heart in the mouth" time to see them both disappearing down the road! But seriously, we need to let our young ones fly the nest.

That might ring true for young adults physically moving out of your home, but it could also apply if they don't follow the faith you have brought them up in. They will return occasionally, but I recommend praying for them when they don't. I firmly believe God hears our prayers. The story of the prodigal son can also be called the "waiting father" or, even better, "the running father"! I'm sure he was longing and praying for the return of his son. I also advise holding onto the fact that you have been sowing seeds of love (and perhaps faith) into your children's lives. We might not get to see the harvest of that sowing, but the Bible tells us to trust God.

"Now faith is confidence in what we hope for and assurance about what we do not see" (Hebrews 11:1).

Articulate

Hats off to the people in the public eye, whether from a career on stage, in film, music, or sport, for example, who can share their vulnerabilities despite the risk of being judged on social media. If well-known folk can use their public persona to articulate the challenges and reality behind the fame and worldly signs of success, then that can be a force for good. Being open, vulnerable and honest about real life is a weakness in the eyes of some. Still, it can have a considerable impact on others.

Being Careful with Anger

It is believed that the nineteenth-century American writer, Ambrose Bierce, first coined this phrase: "Speak when you are angry, and you'll make the best speech you will ever regret." Wise words, indeed. Suffice it to say, it is best practice to pause a moment before we use angry words, even though, at times, it is the proper response in some situations. Occasionally, it is more about a lack of patience or understanding or being unhappy about something else that makes us use words in anger — often in children's hearing.

Who Is Listening to You?

In his book 'Maybe Today', my husband, Tony Miles, writes: "An inconsiderate driver had parked across a pavement, forcing a dad to step into the road with his little girl in a pushchair. The man was not happy with the motorist. He was protective of his daughter, who had been exposed to danger on a busy street due to thoughtless obstruction. However, as the man remonstrated with the van driver, his voice became increasingly raised, and he poured out a torrent of vicious four-letter words and other vulgarities. The youngster looked frightened and tried to interrupt by asking why he was shouting. Her father's reply wasn't much better! I watched the child being pushed off vigorously into the distance. She was evidently confused and upset."

Children are vulnerable to being hurt by our unthinking words and actions. The little girl's dad thought he was shielding her from harm, yet he had put her at risk of being traumatised and scarred by his frightening and abusive language."

"Set a guard over my mouth, Lord;
Keep watch over the door of my lips"
(Psalm 141:3).

Apologies and Forgiveness

I suppose I am a caricature of the Brit who says sorry a lot of the time, even when it's not my fault. I have, on more than one occasion, uttered with a little laugh, "Oops, sorry!" when someone turned a corner in the supermarket and hit my shopping trolley with theirs. I think we do get ridiculed a bit for that. It's strange because there is a deeper issue around saying sorry, and that is that it can be very hard to admit we are wrong about something.

A hugely popular movie released in 1970 was 'Love Story'. It was a moving and ultimately tear-jerking story of an attractive young couple who begin their love story together. The thread throughout the film was "Love means never having to say you're sorry." That's very romantic, but after being married for many years, I know that isn't true. But it isn't always easy — especially when pride and a sense of rightness come into the mix or when you feel truly and deeply hurt. Although sometimes tricky, forgiving someone can be a release and bring peace.

A teenager had fallen out with her best friend two years earlier, and their relationship had not been the same since. The young Christian felt God was prompting her to approach her friend and say sorry. It was time to set things right again. Amazingly, despite the length of time and the depth of hurt, her friend warmly accepted the apology, and the relationship was restored.

Asking for and giving forgiveness are deeply personal choices and not always appropriate. But if the time is right and we feel like we're being nudged to do it, perhaps God is prompting us. If that is the case, then I believe that the Lord will soften hearts as He did with the teenage friends to enable restoration to occur.

Jesus taught His followers how to pray (commonly known as "The Lord's Prayer"). It begins with "Our Father" (The Greek is "Pater", probably the translation of the Aramaic word "Abba" – an intimate term for God, like "Daddy"). The prayer reminds us of the need to ask forgiveness from God and others. Jesus said: "If you forgive other people when they sin against you, your heavenly Father will also forgive you. But if you do not forgive others their sins, your Father will not forgive your sins" (Matthew 6:14–15).

In his book 'A Little Child Shall Lead Them', Johann Christoph Arnold writes about the importance of adults learning from the forgiving spirit of children: "Jesus also calls for a forgiving heart. He speaks of forgiving our brother seventy times seven. Here again, it is children and childlike people who are often far ahead of us... Any adult who has ever asked a child's forgiveness will have experienced how readily and unconditionally a child can forgive."[18]

Mother Theresa said, "If we really want to love, we must learn how to forgive."

A "Proper Goodbye"

I heard of a father who was unexpectedly widowed just a few days after the birth of his triplets. He was comforted by knowing that he and his wife had a "proper goodbye" when he last saw her, despite them not knowing that would be the final time. Since then, he has resolved to give his parents and friends a "proper goodbye" when leaving them. This is a fantastic idea. None of us know when it will be the last time.

A Thought for Today
Tell Them

- This follows nicely from my previous words, but this is a plea to tell people you love them before it's too late. What's the point of waiting to give heartfelt tributes at a funeral when the person concerned hasn't been told how special they were and how much they meant to you before they passed away?

None of us knows how much time we have left or how many opportunities we will have to tell someone we love them. "Carpe diem" is one of the mottos I try to live by: "Seize the day!"

I have probably left many unanswered questions. You might disagree with some points. In that case, thank you for your persistence! Let's explore some more.

FRANCES MILES

Chapter 12
"I Just Don't Know"

You might be reading this book and want to respond:

"It is all very well for you to share these stories and have these ideas, but I have been badly let down in my life; I have been rejected, hurt, abused. I've not known peace or experienced pure, unconditional love. I have lived with fear, violence and disinterest from the grown-ups in my life. This has impacted me as an adult, and I have difficulty forming close relationships."

Or perhaps: "I feel rootless; I didn't have a place to call my home, living with different family members throughout my childhood. I was given no boundaries or structure to live by and have never felt secured by love."

You might say: "I don't know this God whom you talk about because the idea of Him as a Father is simply too much for me to bear. I am hurt and wounded by the father figure I had in my life."

Alternatively, you may think, "I have messed up with my family. I have pushed my loved ones away and don't know what to do." Or: "I fell out with my siblings and have barely spoken to them in years. We had a disagreement, and I cannot bring myself to forgive or forget. Too much water has gone under the bridge, and I will not be the one to make the first move."

You could be experiencing feelings of disappointment, guilt and regret: "I have failed myself, my children, (or those in my care) by the way I have treated them. They deserve the love, respect, time and patience that I, for whatever reason or excuse, could not provide them with."

These scenarios and expressions are not easy to contemplate or dismiss out of hand. Although they aren't my experience, they may be your story. It may be that your memories and experiences aren't as deep, sharp, or impactful as described; however, you still have some doubts and regrets about the past and wish you could turn back the clock to be a better person. I am not offering to solve all the scenarios I have described here. I would suggest visiting a Christian counsellor (or any other respected/recommended counsellor) to help, if that is appropriate for you.

The universal truth is that we are all sinful; we have all done and continue to do things wrong. None of us will always get it right in our relationships, whether at work, college, church, or amongst friends or family. There is some good news for each one of us, too!

The Bible repeatedly tells us that we can have hope despite our failures. The book of Romans 3:23 states, "...for all have sinned and fallen short of the glory of God."

It goes on to say: "...and all are justified freely by His grace through the redemption that came by Christ Jesus."

That means we don't have to strive in our own strength. I believe when Jesus died on the cross, He took away our sin and shame. He also gave the Holy Spirit to fill our hearts, reassure us that we belong to God and bring healing and wholeness. In other words, it's not all about what I have or haven't done. It is about grace. "God's Riches At Christ's Expense" is a helpful way for me to remember what that means. That is what the gospel is all about. Sometimes, religion gets a bad name. That is often justified because being "religious", for the sake of it, can be like a neatly wrapped box with nothing inside.

I came across this anonymous, rather insightful summary of the Christian faith:

Religion: "I've messed up. My Dad is going to kill me."

Gospel: "I've messed up. I need to call my Dad."

"Daddy, Where Are You?"

When our son was three, he and his dad were in the garden. They were "doing work" and Jonathan was busy helping with a rake and gathering leaves. He was having a whale of a time, lost in his own world.

All was fine until my husband bent down behind a bush to wrestle with a determined weed. It was then that our son looked over his shoulder for reassurance and discovered Daddy was nowhere to be seen. Thinking he was alone and abandoned, he froze in panic. Tears trickled down his little face, and he ran towards the house crying, "Daddy, where are you? Don't leave me out here!"

Of course, my husband still had his eye on him. He jumped up and ran towards our little boy, sweeping him into his arms. "It's all right, I'm here. Daddy wouldn't leave you alone."

It Was A Good Friday

Earlier in the book, I shared the story of the young child at the football match. He had lost his daddy and was upset. I found it so profound, as this happened on Good Friday, a day when Christians mark one of the most significant events on our calendar — when Jesus of Nazareth was nailed to a cross to die.

Although I believe He was without sin, He died for the sins of everyone — including you, including me. Through the searing pain and with the weight of the world on His shoulders, Jesus cries out in desperation and loss: "My God, My God, why have You forsaken me?" (Mark 15:34)

But when Jesus came to the very end of His earthly life, He used a well-known prayer, often said before going to sleep (Psalm 31:5 — "Into Your hands I commit My Spirit."). Jesus, however, at that most significant of moments, added an extra word, "Father", at the beginning of that final prayer. Jesus at His most desolate. On a cross, killed for crimes He didn't commit. An innocent man, with love streaming from His hands and feet, called out to God to forgive those who were responsible for His death. Jesus wasn't angry with His Father for allowing this to happen; instead, He acknowledged and trusted Him until He breathed His last (Luke 23:46).

Abba, Father

In her book 'Rooted in Love — Lent Reflections on Life in Christ', Bishop Sarah Mullally collected meditations from bishops in the London area.[19] One of those, written by Graham Tomlin, refers to the phrase 'Abba', an intimate and familiar word, which Jesus often used when praying to the Father. As God's only Son, Jesus is rightly allowed to use this title, yet Tomlin notes... "it seemed that in the earliest churches, Christians were already calling God Abba in their prayer and worship."

Although God loves the whole world, He longs for a relationship with each of us as individuals. Because of what Jesus did on the cross, we can become adopted sons and daughters in His family if we receive His love and forgiveness.

Guilt, disappointment, anger and sadness are all feelings we can legitimately express. Alternatively, we might keep them locked up inside when we feel like we have been let down or abandoned. We might lose sight of the fact that there is a God who is our Heavenly Father.

It is perhaps too simple an analogy, but the sun is always there; even though the light can be hidden by clouds or heavy fog. I believe God is there, too. We must trust that He is and loves us despite our wrongdoings. Best of all, if we turn to Him to say sorry, just like that prodigal son who returned to His dad, God is there waiting to embrace us with His love and enfold us in His forgiveness and peace.

Jesus heard those words of belonging, love and affirmation at His baptism. We will discover that He heard the words again from God — with a small group of His followers around Him to witness it, too. This was during an event called the Transfiguration. How much more do we also need reassurance?

We might be blessed to know our parents and can trace our family tree or be even more blessed to have had a good relationship with our relatives. I suggest, however, that God, our Heavenly Father, can do so much more than a human family can ever do.

"See what great love the Father has lavished on us, that we should be called children of God! And that is what we are!" (1 John 3:1)

Even though my story is one of stability and love throughout my childhood, I still had that doubt lingering in my mind. I do not believe that I would have coped too well with that or life in general without faith in a loving and trustworthy God. However, I did need to make sure that my faith was my own and not just inherited from my parents.

A few years ago, I went through a challenging time and experienced periods of self-doubt, anxiety and uncertainty. But thanks to the support of my husband and the encouragement of family and friends, I learnt to lean into and entirely depend upon God, who is full of love and mercy. When I was emerging from this difficult season, I sensed that a burden that had been weighing heavily on me was lifted and I felt so much lighter. That was an answer to my earnest prayer. God is good! He wants the best for us. He is all we need to know how loved we are and how we can be truly ourselves and fully forgiven. This gives me the assurance that with God, I know I am rooted, loved and affirmed in Him.

Earlier in the book, I mentioned that my special pen had gone missing. Well, I still haven't found it, despite my continuing searching! I am reminded that as well as the parable of the Lost Son, which I explored in chapter four ("Whom I Love"), the writer Luke also included two other stories Jesus told about searching and finding. He spoke out in response to the mumblings from religious leaders and teachers who complained that He welcomed sinners and ate with them. We have the story of the shepherd who loses one sheep and leaves the 99 behind to search for the one. The Bible tells us: "And when he finds it, he joyfully puts it on his shoulders and goes home" (Luke 15:5–6).

Then, there is the woman who has ten silver coins, but she loses one. So, she lights a lamp, sweeps the house, and searches carefully until she finds it. She gathers her neighbours together with her friends to rejoice with her. If I ever find my pen, I might do the same! Jesus told these three stories to illustrate that

God is like a good shepherd, seeking us out in love. He is beyond delighted when just one person realises they need God and comes to Him asking for forgiveness.

St Augustine was the Bishop of Hippo (now "Annaba" in Algeria) from 396 to 430 AD. Before all that, Augustine was known to be rebellious and strong-willed, and despite being encouraged into faith by his mother, he instead lived extravagantly and put other things before God. After turning to Christianity, Augustine wrote 'Confessions', an autobiographical work consisting of 13 books retelling his childhood, early adulthood and the story of his conversion. He described it rather beautifully like this: "Almighty God, You have made us for Yourself, and our hearts are restless until they find their rest in You."[20] I wonder if that resonates with you as much as it does with me.

The prolific hymn writer Charles Wesley (brother of John) wrote more than 6,500 hymns in the eighteenth century. This was after both brothers had an extraordinary encounter with God. Though they had faith before then, it was all cerebral, and it wasn't until they had experienced an overwhelming sense of the love and presence of God that it took root in their hearts and souls, too. Wesley's hymns remain popular in churches around the world today. The words and music relate to the reality of our human condition and our necessity for God:

"Love divine, all loves excelling,

Joy of heaven to earth come down."

A Thought for Today
Someone To Hold Onto

*"The Lord is close to the broken-hearted
and saves those who are crushed in spirit"
(Psalm 34:18).*

- Why not reach out to Him today? He loves you — even you — despite your doubts and uncertainties.

FRANCES MILES

Chapter 13
Words of Affirmation: A Second Time

"After six days Jesus took with Him Peter, James and John the brother of James, and led them up a high mountain by themselves. There, He was transfigured before them. His face shone like the sun, and His clothes became as white as the light. Just then, Moses and Elijah appeared before them, talking with Jesus. Peter said to Jesus, 'Lord, it is good for us to be here. If you wish, I will put up three shelters — one for You, one for Moses and one for Elijah.' While he was still speaking, a bright cloud covered them, and a voice from the cloud said, 'This is My Son, whom I love; with Him, I am well pleased. Listen to Him!'" (Matthew 17:1–5)

Widening the Circle

According to the Bible, Jesus didn't frequently hear words said out loud from God, but the synoptic Gospel writers recorded two instances of an audible voice.

As we have been reflecting, the first time was at Jesus' baptism. On that occasion, it was just Jesus and John the Baptiser. But it happens again, with other witnesses this time — when the same words giving Jesus a seal of approval are said — but with a small but significant addition. This is called the Transfiguration, where Jesus is transfigured; His appearance changes and His clothes become radiant.

Jesus was with His closest friends: Peter, John and James. According to tradition, identified by Origen in the third century, they climbed Mount Tabor in Israel. During this incredible moment, the men saw Moses and Elijah, who appeared before them and talked with Jesus. They hear a voice from the cloud: the Father affirming His love and approval of His Son.

This time, the disciples are charged to listen to Jesus. God could be declaring that the older world of Moses and Elijah has passed. Now, Jesus is bringing the Kingdom of God in a new and more powerful way.

The Transfiguration occurs when Jesus is preparing Himself and His disciples for what is on the horizon — the cross. I wonder what the impact was on these three men — and on Jesus, who heard again His Father's love and affirmation of who He was before He set the course for His death. God was delighted and proud of Him.

I have previously mentioned David Mathis, a Pastor and executive editor of John Piper's website ("desiringgod.org"). In his February 21 blog, entitled 'This is my Beloved Son', Mathis writes: "The transfiguration may give us as profound a peek into a father's love for his son as we can find... Soon, Jesus will face the cross, and be surrounded by mockers and the power of darkness."[21] Mathis quotes the theologian Donald Macleod in his book 'Christ Crucified': "...but here, in the calm before the storm, it is as if his Father says, 'Son, in all you are now going to face, never forget who you are, never forget that I love you, and never forget how proud I am of you.'"[22]

Stabilising Words

Mathis concludes: "God wired the souls of men to hear and be stabilised by such words of identity, love and approval from their fathers. This is why it can be so deeply painful for sons whose fathers have been negligent, or worse, with their words. And why it is no small thing, in Christ, to find a Father in heaven who speaks to His Son — and sons — as He does."

The apostle Peter later described his experience when he wrote to his fellow believers: "For we did not follow cleverly devised stories when we told you about the coming of our Lord Jesus Christ in power, but we were eyewitnesses of His majesty. He received honour and glory from God the Father when the voice came to Him from the Majestic Glory, saying, 'This is My Son, whom I love; with Him I am well pleased.' We ourselves heard this voice that came from heaven when we were with Him on the sacred mountain" (2 Peter 1:16–18).

I was discussing my book with a friend who was interested in what I was writing. He was going through a very painful situation in his own family and asked me, "So what is the answer?" It's an excellent question. No family is perfect, despite appearances to the contrary. There are hurt feelings, painful memories and tricky relationships to manage.

Ultimately, however, my response is that we humans don't possess the complete answer within our own power or strength. Even if you apply all the principles of this book, there is still no guarantee that life will be easy or that all relationship issues will be resolved successfully. But I am convinced that it can make a difference. Moreover, even when the worst happens, God holds you in His love. God has shown us He can be our perfect parent and provide us with all the love, stability and well-being we need.

A Thought for Today
And To Keep Forever

God loved His son deeply, yet we are told in John 3:16 that He loved the world "so much" too. This is the sacrifice He had to make: "He who did not spare His own Son, but gave Him up for us all how will He not also, along with Him, graciously give us all things?" (Romans 8:32)

FRANCES MILES

Conclusion

"Humanity owes the child the best it has to give."
Eglantyne Jebb, Founder of Save the Children

We still have so much to do. We don't have to look too far to see the impact of conflict, turmoil, the climate crisis and migration on the younger generation. Before we point the finger at governments and global leaders, maybe the pages of this book have prompted us to look a little closer to home: to the hardness of our hearts or to examine how we treat those we call "our family".

I have mentioned that there were twenty years of exploration before I sat down to write. I was repeatedly taken aback by how many times the same threads and themes were woven into the stories I encountered. This confirmed to me that whatever our creed, race, background, or status, there is a universal need within us for strong foundations; to know we are loved and to be noticed and understood.

If we can resolve to demonstrate love and kindness wherever possible each day, that's one thing. However, perhaps by reflecting on our childhoods and upbringing, we can also take steps to help make amends for past wrongs. That is for you to decide.

Seeking the Truth

I'm not sure why it took until I was in my sixth decade to ask my mum and dad my "Were you disappointed when I was born?" question. I wanted to know the answer, but at the same time, I didn't.

Do you have something that has been eating away at you? Maybe the time is right to ask the question of your heart, write someone a letter, pick up the phone to apologise to someone or send a message to a friend, letting them know you are thinking about them and praying for them.

But I also believe we shouldn't try to do this alone. God, who loves you and me, knows you; you are precious to Him. God knows us better than we know ourselves! Nothing we can do can make God love us more... or less.

Some might say, "I'm hiding from myself, there are things I don't want to confront, and I won't open up to others for fear of being hurt." The Bible makes it clear that we will have to give an account of ourselves to God (1 Corinthians 4:5). If we open our hearts to our Heavenly Father through His Son Jesus and with the help of the Holy Spirit, we can be adopted into God's family. In 2 Corinthians 5:17–21, Paul explains that being "in Christ" results in a person becoming a "new creation". It is our new identity. God says: "You, Frances (insert your name), are My daughter," or "You (insert your name) are My son."

Some might say: "I am unlovable, and I am a lost cause. I hate myself because of what was said to me in the past or because of what I have done to others." The Bible says God loved us so much He sent His Son Jesus to die for us on the cross. We are genuinely and deeply loved.

Some of us might say, "I was told I was a mistake" or "I have no gifts to offer. I am not skilled in any way," we can learn that each of us is unique and special. God says to the young Jeremiah, "Before I formed you in the womb, I knew you" (Jeremiah 1:5).

Some of us might say, "I just can't make a success of my life. I am depressed and confused because I feel so unwanted and neglected by others." Jesus said: "So don't be afraid; you are worth more than many sparrows" (Matthew 10:31).

The Man On the Bus: A Reflection

A man with tattoos and a football shirt was waiting at the bus stop. As he got onto my bus, he was speaking loudly and slowly on his phone. I assumed he was arguing with another person. I felt uneasy at that moment, perhaps an unwilling witness to an escalating situation.

After a while, it became apparent that this man was, in fact, speaking to an older person or perhaps a small child. "I love you; I love you!" he earnestly declared as he ended the call.

Boy, what a relief! I had been foolishly jumping to conclusions. But I also asked myself why I was taken aback that this man declared his love so publicly. Maybe it's because we don't often hear that phrase aloud — we might write it in a text message or a Valentine's card. It made me wonder if I said "I love you" enough to my family or close friends.

I was reminded of this when I travelled to a Good Friday church service. The "I Love You" phrase echoed in my heart and mind — the image of Jesus in anguish on a cross with outstretched arms burned into my soul. The best demonstration of God's "I love you" was through the sacrifice of His Son. I pondered what this all meant to me, my family, a hurting world, and the man on the bus.

"I love you," God whispers to me. "Thank you," I respond on bended knees.

Thank you, too, for journeying with me. As I share this message, I have tried to faithfully convey what was laid on my heart so many years ago. My search for an answer from my parents was meaningful to me. Still, I know that for many, their quests and uncertainties aren't always easy to resolve. Sometimes, answers won't lead to a resolution.

But I hope and pray that we all will come to believe that you and I are of more value than we could ever know. We don't have to prove ourselves to God. He sees, loves, and deeply knows us. I pray you may know this for yourself so that you will be encouraged and inspired to move forward with confidence and empowered to face life's challenges with strength and grace.

Returning to the reflection at the beginning of the book:

"I love trees with those hidden roots; they remind me of the anchors in my life that make me feel secure, allowing me to stand resolute against the storms of life."

'Rooted, Loved, Affirmed' — imperfect lives encountering Perfect Love.

References

[1] 'The Gift' Series 2, chapter 1. BBC Sounds. Broadcast on 6 November 2024. Available at: https://www.bbc.co.uk/sounds/play/m0024p01

[2] Calvin Miller, 'The Singer'. First edition 1975, Inter-Varsity Christian Fellowship.

[3] Dougal Shaw BBC News 'If You Die Early, How Will Your Children Remember You?' 5 March 2019. Available at: https://www.bbc.co.uk/news/stories-47334604. Accessed November 2024.

[4] David Mathis, 'This is My Beloved Son', 5 February 2021. Available at: https://www.desiringgod.org/articles/this-is-my-beloved-son

[5] Stewardship. Available at: https://www.stewardship.org.uk

[6] BBC Radio 4 Desert Island Discs., 25 March 2022. Available at: https://www.bbc.co.uk/programmes/m0015ksq Accessed, 2023.

[7] Elton John. 'Me'. Macmillan 2019.

[8] SoundAndVision. 'Brian May's Father Disappointment Until "Madison Square Garden" Happened'. 15 October 2023. Available at: https://youtu.be/tdBJPaMbsno?si=K6Wmnyil4J5SPtqN   Accessed 2023.

[9] Extract from: Kevin Maher, 'David Beckham Waited 20 Years For Any Praise From His Dad. I Know Why'; The Times, 25 March 2024.

[10] P. Fontaine, taken from Tony Castle's book, 'Quotations For All Occasions', Marshall Pickering 1989.

[11] Ian Wright, 'Overcoming the Odds', BBC iPlayer, first broadcast May 2021. Available at: https://www.youtube.com/watch?v=6caCqn_nD6o

[12] David Sedaris. 'Happy-Go-Lucky', Abacus. 1 June 2023.

[13] Phoebe McIndoe, County Lines. Available at: https://www.bbc.co.uk/programmes/m0025d4r 25 November 2024. Accessed November 2024.

[14] Eleanor Anstruther on X. @ellieanstuther (21/04/2023).

[15] BBC Radio 4 Desert Island Discs, 17 September 2023. Available at: https://www.bbc.co.uk/sounds/play/m001qlz2 Accessed 2024.

[16] Nadine White, Independent Newspaper (27 January 2022). Available at: https://www.independent.co.uk/independentpremium/long-reads/barrel-children-windrush-black-families-b1958518.html Accessed 2024.

[17] Steve Mann. 'Will You Join Our Crusade?' Circle Books, 2014.

[18] Cally Magalhães, 'Dancing With Thieves', Sarah Grace Publishing, 2020.

[19] Johann Christoph Arnold. 'A Little Child Shall Lead Them', Inter-Varsity Press, 1997.

[20] Graham Tomlin, quoted in Sarah Mullally's, 'Rooted in Love — Lent Reflections on Life in Christ'. (Chapter 30). SPCK, 2020.

[21] St Augustine. 'Confessions' (Written in Latin between AD 397 and 400.).

[22] David Mathis, 'This is My Beloved Son', 5 February 2021. Available at: https://www.desiringgod.org/articles/this-is-my-beloved-son

[23] Donald Macleod. 'Christ Crucified', IVP Academic, 2014.

ROOTED, LOVED, AFFIRMED

FRANCES MILES

About the Author

Frances was born and raised in Surrey, the third of four children of former Councillor Michael Arthur MBE and his wife, Ann. The family attended Epsom Methodist Church, where Frances met her future husband, Tony. After studying at Cliff College, a Methodist Bible school in the Peak District, she began working in local government. Following their marriage, Frances and Tony relocated to Bristol for Tony's training in the Methodist ministry, after which they moved to Colchester.

In 2005, while living in Loughton, Frances started working for Stewardship, a prominent Christian financial services charity that supports givers, churches and ministries. She became the leader of the Partner Services Division and served on the Senior Leadership Team until December 2021. During her time with the organisation, Frances enjoyed sharing her passion for generosity and demonstrating how ordinary Christians can make a difference.

Since 2022, Frances has focused on supporting her family and volunteering in various roles at her church, as well as serving as secretary of her local Rotary Club. Frances also assists her husband in his role as Superintendent Minister at Methodist Central Hall Westminster, with whom she co-authored a book entitled 'Like a Child'.

Together, they have two adult children and five grandchildren. In her spare time, she delights in spending time with family and friends, enjoying Ronnie Scott's Jazz Club with Tony, watching Fulham FC, attending a weekly dance class, and listening to BBC Radio 4's The Archers.

www.rootedlovedaffirmed.com

Other Books

'Like a Child'

Co-authored by Tony and Frances Miles, published by Rooftops Publishing, 2003. ISBN 0-9544038-0-0

ROOTED, LOVED, AFFIRMED

FRANCES MILES

About PublishU

PublishU enables you to tell your story or communicate your message by writing and publishing a book worldwide.

"I never thought I would be able to write a book, let alone in 100 days... now I'm asking what else have I told myself that I can't do that I actually can?'"

PublishU Author

To find out more visit

www.PublishU.com

Printed in Great Britain
by Amazon